a bright tomorrow

a bright
tomorrow

WORDS

OF WISDOM

FOR THE

DAYS AHEAD

This Billy Graham Library Selection special edition is published by the Billy Graham Evangelistic Association with permission from Crossway Books (a division of Good News Publishers).

A Bright Tomorrow
Copyright © 2001 by Good News Publishers
Published by Crossway Books
        a division of Good News Publishers
        1300 Crescent Street
        Wheaton, Illinois 60187

Book design: Cindy Kiple
First printing 2001
Printed in the United States of America

Unless otherwise designated, Scripture is taken from the *Holy Bible: New International Version®*. Copyright © 1973, 1978, 1984 by International Bible Society. Used by permission of Zondervan Publishing House. All rights reserved.

The "NIV" and "New International Version" trademarks are registered in the United States Patent and Trademark Office by International Bible Society. Use of either trademark requires the permission of International Bible Society.

Scripture references marked NLT are taken from the *Holy Bible, New Living Translation*, copyright © 1996. Used by permission of Tyndale House Publishers, Inc., Wheaton, Ill., 60189. All rights reserved.

LIBRARY OF CONGRESS CATALOGING-IN-PUBLICATION DATA
A bright tomorrow : words of wisdom for the days ahead.
    p.   cm.
  Includes bibliographical references.
  Previously ISBN 1-58134-233-0
  ISBN 0-913367-52-4
  1. Christian life—Quotations, maxims, etc. 2. Spiritual life—
Christianity—Quotations, maxims, etc. I. Crossway Books.
BV4513.B75 2001
242—dc21

contents

Remember your Creator in the days of your youth. . . . Fear God and keep his commandments, for this is the whole duty of man.

ECCLESIASTES 12:1,13

Why Are You Here?

WHAT AN AMAZING
GIFT GOD GIVES EACH
OF US—THE POTENTIAL TO
LIVE OUT OUR CALLINGS
AND PURPOSE TO THE
FULLEST, AWARE OF THE
AMAZING LIFE HE HAS
FOR US, AWARE OF THE
EMPTINESS OF LIFE
WITHOUT HIM.

Nancie Carmichael

The past is prologue. The time of preparation has ended; the task of life awaits. As you ponder the pathway stretching before you, consider: Will you build for time alone, or will you build for eternity? Happy are they indeed who spend themselves for what will last, rather than for things that will ultimately perish. Your Creator has put you in this world to do a specific, unique task— a work no one else can do. Your fulfillment in this life and your eternal reward in heaven depend on finding out what that task is. The very reason you exist is to discover what you were created to be and to do here. Many others have gone before you in this quest for life's meaning. In the following pages saints past and present offer guidance for the road ahead. ❧

Many people in our society are on a seemingly endless and often frantic quest for personal identity and self-worth. Identity crises are common at almost every age level. Superficial love and fractured relationships are but symptoms of our failure to resolve the fundamental issues of who we are, why we exist, and where we're going. Sadly, most people will live and die without ever understanding God's purpose for their lives. . . .

Don't allow sin, Satan, or circumstances to rob you of your sense of identity in Christ. Make it the focus of everything you do. Remember who you are—God's child; why you are here—to serve and glorify Him; and where you are going—heaven, where you will spend eternity in His presence.

John MacArthur

Trust in the LORD with all your heart and lean not on your own understanding; in all your ways acknowledge him, and he will make your paths straight.

Proverbs 3:5-6

Aim your life at God's glory; make it the standard by which you evaluate everything you do.

John MacArthur

a bright
tomorrow

Ascribe to the LORD the glory due his name. Bring an offering and come before him; worship the LORD in the splendor of his holiness.

1 Chronicles 16:29

Jesus entered the world as a servant, and that is what He asks of us— to be servants for His glory and for the increase of God's kingdom.

Ellen Banks Elwell

O Lord, how trivial are my aspirations and desires. I pursue the amusements and toys and carnality of the modern world, while the higher longings of my soul weaken from neglect. What do I need to *remove* from my life, in order to throw myself without reserve or impediment into the great cause of the Gospel? This is my brief moment in history. I do not have forever. Now is my time to speak to my generation. Purify my heart, Lord. Energize my desires. Open my eyes. Compel me with my personal responsibility to serve the interests of the Gospel in the world today. O Lord, let me spend my life for you, disregarding all risks, accepting all consequences. Let the power of the Gospel so grip me that I act upon it, come what may. Let me recover the power to live and to die for my faith. In the holy name of Christ, amen.

Raymond C. Ortlund, Jr.

Never be lacking in zeal, but keep your spiritual fervor, serving the Lord.

Romans 12:11

In true religion, nothing, nothing at all, is more important than wholehearted and unqualified obedience to the words of God.

D. A. Carson

Live today in the confidence that Christ cannot fail. He will always accomplish His purposes.

John MacArthur

Our great mission in the church is to love, learn, and live to call men and women to Jesus Christ. As a believer who truly desires to glorify God and honor His supreme will and purpose, you will share God's love for the lost and share in His mission to redeem them. Christ came into the world to bring sinners to Himself for His and the Father's glory. As Christ's representative, you are sent into the world with the same purpose—to bring glory and honor to God.

John MacArthur

a bright tomorrow

*A*s I look back on some of the "roads not taken," I realize it was my Christian heritage that weighed in back where the roads forked. In my mid-twenties I was trying to choose my life partner. On the same weekend in November one fellow I was dating told me he loved me, and the other fellow I was dating asked me to marry him.

Both were intelligent, tall, handsome, witty, and charming. The first fellow was quite successful already. Our times together were spent at country clubs, elegant parties, and lovely dinners. The second fellow was scrimping by in seminary, and our time together was spent over a bucket of chicken on a study date—he writing papers and I preparing lecture notes for the high school classes I taught.

The first fellow and I did not share the same spiritual heritage or level of commitment, but the second one and I did. In fact, his level of commitment was greater than mine at the time and required a great deal of sacrifice. He wanted to teach and train Christians on the mission field. The lap of luxury looked much more appealing than a vow of poverty. But . . . when it came down to making a decision, I could not walk into the future and not share my past. After trusting Christ, it was the biggest decision I ever made.

We still get the bucket of chicken, and many nights are study nights. . . . But the blessings flowing from that decision are a source of profound and continuing joy.

LAEL F. ARRINGTON

How can we pray for God's purpose for our lives? As a teenager at missionary services in our local church, I would sing with the congregation, "I'll go where you want me to go, dear Lord/O'er mountain, o'er plain, o'er sea./I'll be what you want me to be, dear Lord." . . . Now with life changing at a dizzying rate, I pray, "Lord, refresh my passion to live wholeheartedly for You!" There is no greater purpose than simply to be aware of the need to share what we have received. Our world is hungry for the priceless treasure, Jesus. . . . Pray that the Lord will show you needs in which you can best fulfill your purpose, and prayerfully consider how God can use you there. He does want to use you, and sometimes it takes awhile to find out exactly how and where.

Nancie Carmichael

I have agonized over the will of God. Recently I took a look back over the years of my life. I realized that who I am today is the result of all the decisions I have made until now. I am the result of hundreds of thousands of decisions, many of which did not seem very important at the time. . . . But taken together they have made me exactly who I am today. The same is true for all of us. You make your decisions, and then your decisions turn around and make you.

Ray Pritchard

One reason many of us . . . are not seeing God actively at work in our lives is that we are still giving Him our leftovers and expecting Him to be satisfied. What He wants is to be first in everything.

When we give God any lesser priority in our lives, we are relegating the Owner to the demeaning position *below* that of His steward or manager. That's never going to work because it doesn't work on the human level. Your employer would not be satisfied with your leftover time, energy, and skills.

Neither is God. You can give God a million dollars, but if it's out of your leftovers, He finds it unacceptable. That's the principle of priority we need to understand.

Tony Evans

Employers expect the undivided loyalty of their staff, and we think them entitled to do so. But how much stronger is God's claim! Do we give our God the resolute, wholehearted allegiance for which He asks, and which is His due? Does He really come first in our lives?

What will it mean in practice for me to put God first? This much, at least. All the 101 things I have to do each day, and the 101 demands on me which I know I must try to meet, will all be approached as ventures of loving service to Him, and I shall do the best I can in everything for his sake—which attitude, as George Herbert quaintly said, "makes drudgery divine. . . ."

And then I shall find that, through the secret work of the Spirit, which is known by its effects, my very purpose of pleasing God gives me new energy for all these tasks and relationships, energy which otherwise I could not have had. . . . Self-absorbed resentments dissolve, and zest for life, happiness in doing things, and love for others all grow great when God comes first.

So wake up, enthrone your God—and *live!*

J. I. Packer

Expectation is the child of prayer and faith, and is owned of the Lord as an acceptable grace. We should desire nothing but what would be right for God to give, and then our expectation would be all from God; and concerning really good things we should not look to second causes, but to the Lord alone, and so again our expectation should be all from Him. The vain expectations of worldly men come not; they promise, but there is no performance; our expectations are on the way, and in due season will arrive to satisfy our hopes. Happy is the man who feels that all he has, all he wants, and all he expects are to be found in His God.

C. H. Spurgeon

a   b r i g h t
       t o m o r r o w

When we follow Christ, we have new priorities. Second
Corinthians 5:17 says, "If anyone is in Christ, he is a new creation;
the old has gone, the new has come!" He turns everything in our
lives upside down! We don't fit Him into our daily planner, as
everything pales before knowing Him as Lord. We become aware
that we are part of a wonderful family—with a loving, good Father
at the head, with Jesus Christ the Cornerstone, and with the Holy
Spirit as guide and counselor. Often we are afraid of giving all to
Christ—perhaps afraid of losing control. But He says, "Come to
me, all you who are weary and burdened, and I will give you rest.
Take my yoke upon you and learn from me. . . . For my yoke is
easy and my burden is light."

Nancie Carmichael

It would be an honor to be an ambassador of the United States,
representing this country's power and capabilities to other
countries. But you have an even greater honor—to represent the
power and capabilities of the living God. . . . Because you are in
Christ, you have glorious privileges that include union with God,
access to the Father, security, affection, dominion, possession,
holiness, illumination, and compassion. What greater honor can

there be than to proclaim the excellencies of the one who has granted you such marvelous privileges?

John MacArthur

Just as framing shapes a house, and a skeleton is the shape of a human body, certain important choices shape your life and my life. The framing years, driven by passion and maybe a little bit of insanity, seem to go fast. It seems that it's in the young adult years where we make life-shaping choices, often at an accelerated rate— where to attend higher education (if at all), what work to pursue, whom to marry (if one marries), how many children to have, and where to live. These are important, life-shaping choices.

But there are choices we make that are much more subtle and yet just as influential. They are the decisions of the spirit and of the will that ultimately shape our lives, our belief systems that form our character throughout life.

Nancie Carmichael

But be very careful to keep the commandment and the law that Moses the servant of the LORD gave you: to love the LORD your God, to walk in all his ways, to obey his commands, to hold fast to him and to serve him with all your heart and all your soul.

Joshua 22:5

It's been said that some Christians are so heavenly minded, they're no earthly good. But usually the opposite is true. Many Christians are so enamored with this present world that they no longer look forward to heaven. They have everything they want right here. The health, wealth, and prosperity doctrine has convinced them that Christians can have it all, so they pursue "the good life" with a vengeance. . . .

[God] extends to us all the rights and privileges of our heavenly citizenship. Let that assurance encourage you today to live to His glory and to rely on His heavenly provisions. Take care not to let impure aspirations or trivial pursuits distract you from your heavenly priorities.

John MacArthur

When God redeemed you, He not only forgave your trespasses and removed the guilt and penalty of sin, but He also gave you spiritual wisdom and insight—two essential elements for godly living. Together they speak of the ability to understand God's will and apply it to your life in practical ways.

As a believer, you understand the most sublime truths of all. For example, you know that God created the world and controls the course of history. You know that mankind's reason for existence is to know and glorify Him. You have goals and priorities that transcend earthly circumstances and limitations.

John MacArthur

One of the main reasons people do not understand or experience the sovereignty of grace and the way it works through the awakening of sovereign joy is that their hunger and thirst for God is so small. . . . [T]hey do not long for anything very much. They are just coasting. They are not passionate about anything. They are "cold," not just toward the glory of Christ in the Gospel, but toward everything. Even their sins are picked at rather than swallowed with passion. . . . But alongside prayer, the remedy for people without passion and without hunger and thirst for God is to display God Himself as infinitely more desirable—more satisfying—than all creation.

John Piper

You have two choices. You can spend your life chasing idols your hands have made. (But when you die, your idols die with you.) Or you can spend your life doing God's will. Then when you die, it's not over. Life has just begun!

Ray Pritchard

I am the LORD your God, who teaches you what is best for you, who directs you in the way you should go.

ISAIAH 48:17

a bright

God's Blueprint for Your Life

tomorrow

GOD ASKS US TO

SEEK HIS GUIDANCE

AND THEN SERVE HIM

ACCORDING TO HIS

PLANS, NOT OUR OWN.

Sheila Cragg

When Jesus walked among us here on earth, He repeatedly stated His life purpose: "I have come to do your will, O God" (Hebrews 10:7). He told the crowds that followed Him from place to place, "I have come down from heaven not to do my will but to do the will of him who sent me" (John 6:38). He prayed in the garden, "Not my will, but yours be done." After His resurrection, He appeared to His disciples and told them, "As the Father has sent me, I am sending you" (John 20:21). We, His twenty-first-century disciples, are now being sent by Jesus to find and do our Father's will. Let us listen carefully to Him and then obey.

If God has enough wisdom to manage the boundaries of the sea, the motions of the heavens, and the instincts of the animals, He has more than enough wisdom to run your life. To quote from Thomas Boston, "To this wise God we may safely entrust all our concerns, knowing He will manage them all so as to promote His own glory and our real good."

Philip Graham Ryken

It's been wisely said that trying to improve on God's plan is more pretentious than trying to improve the *Mona Lisa* with an ink pen. All you'd do is ruin the masterpiece.

John MacArthur

Even when we think we are heading toward God, without His guidance we don't have a clue. Whether we are men or women, young or old, experienced drivers or novice travelers, we are born without the inclination or the capacity to ask for directions. It is . . . a sin-induced blindness to God. The only way we can find our way home is with His guidance, for without it, we are flying blind.

David Haney

t's a myth that God makes His will hard to find. Many people struggle unnecessarily in this area. Perhaps they are seeking 100 percent certainty, or maybe they are seeking some kind of message from God—a postcard that reads, "Dear Jack: Buy the red Pontiac. Signed, God." Or they fear that one night, while they are watching Monday Night Football, *God will reveal His will, and they will somehow miss it. Or they worry that they have sinned too much and have blown their only chance to do God's will.*

To all these things God says, "Trust Me." God wants you to know His will more than you want to know it. . . . He takes full responsibility for getting you from here to there step by step. He has said, "Never will I leave you" (Hebrews 13:5). And He won't. He also said, "I will instruct you and teach you in the way you should go" (Psalm 32:8). And He will. He also promised, "Surely I will be with you always" (Matthew 28:20). And He is.

We think that God's will is hard to find. The biblical perspective is quite different. God will reveal His will to anyone who is willing to do it. That leads me to one final thought: God ordinarily will not show you His will in order for you to consider it. He won't show you His will so you can say, "Maybe I will . . . maybe I won't. How about Plan B, Lord?". . . . If you want to know God's will, you have to choose to do it before you know what it is.

RAY PRITCHARD

God's will is a relationship, not a location. It is not a question of where you should go or what you should do. Knowing the will of God is not primarily about whom you should marry or when you should get married. It's not about taking this job or that job, or how many kids you should have, or where you should go to school, or whether you should be a missionary or not. Those are secondary questions. The primary question is: Are you willing to stay close to God and follow wherever He leads you?

Ray Pritchard

In a time of change and crisis, we need to be much in prayer, not only on our knees, but in that sweet form of inward prayer, in which the spirit is constantly offering itself up to God, asking to be shown His will. . . . Wrapped in prayer like this, the trustful believer may tread the deck of the ocean steamer night after night, sure that He who points the stars to their courses will not fail to direct the soul which has no other aim than to do His will.

One good form of prayer at such a juncture is to ask that doors may be shut, that the way may be closed, and that all enterprises that are not according to God's will may be arrested at their beginning.

F. B. Meyer

a bright
tomorrow

How does God guide His people? A thousand different ways. But no matter what form the guidance may take, it will always be 100 percent consistent with the Word of God, because God does not contradict Himself. God's moment-by-moment leading comes through a variety of means. Sometimes through the advice of good Christian friends. Sometimes through prayer. Sometimes by listening to a sermon. Sometimes by an inner conviction that God has spoken to us. Sometimes by a deep sense of inner peace. Sometimes God will guide us through a particular passage of Scripture. Sometimes all of the circumstances of life clearly point in one direction. Sometimes He simply gives us the wisdom to make the right decision. Sometimes He "speaks" to us. Sometimes He guides us by His silence. Very often it is a combination of all of these things put together.

God is committed to guiding His children on their journey from earth to heaven. And though His methods may change, and though sometimes they may be difficult to understand, God is committed to seeing that you ultimately reach your final destination.

Ray Pritchard

For this God is our God for ever and ever; he will be our guide even to the end.

Psalm 48:14

If you trust God absolutely, it is for Him to give you clear directions as to what you should do. And when the time for action arrives, He will have given you such unmistakable indications of His will that you will not be able to mistake them or err therein.

F. B. Meyer

If the God of providence is calling someone to a particular ministry, He will so overrule that person's situation that he or she will be able to move into that ministry. If circumstances make such a move impossible, the right conclusion is that though God indeed has a ministry for this person, it is not what was originally thought, because of the way the door of circumstances has been closed.

J. I. Packer

Only Christ can open doors leading into God's will. He alone has the keys. When our circumstances seem to be most impossible, that is when God most delights to open doors for His people. This demands that we pray to Him alone who can open the door to effective ministry. . . . God's open doors are only seen with the eyes of faith. Natural eyes see only the impossibilities. Physical eyes see only the obstacles. Only spiritual eyes can see God's doors opening before us. Only faith can see God-given opportunities.

Steven J. Lawson

We have gone along from day to day, not trying to make plans too definitely, but rather hoping indeed that His plans would be our only plan. The way has been sweet, and our hearts have been glad, except as we view our own coldness of heart and habit of returning to the old ways. Indeed we have much to unlearn by His grace.

Francis Schaeffer

Those who are the sons of God will be led by the Spirit of God. That is to say, those who have been adopted, those who are God's children, will be guided in their lives and in their decisions by the Spirit of God. This is both the promise and the proof of a true relationship with God.

David Haney

Wait for God! We are too feverish, too hasty, too impatient. It is a great mistake. Everything comes only to those who can wait. "They that wait on the Lord shall inherit the earth." . . . Now turn your heart to God; accept His will; tell Him that you leave to Him the realization of your dream. "Wait on the Lord, and keep His way, and He shall exalt thee to inherit the land."

F. B. Meyer

Let's face the truth—we want to know the future. At least we think we do. We want to know what is going to happen next year so we can be ready in advance. But God won't play that game with us. . . .

Let's be clear on this one point: it is *rarely* God's will for you to know your personal future. Psalm 119:105 paints a clear picture of how we discover the will of God: "Your word is a lamp to my feet and a light for my path." The picture here is not of a blazing light that illuminates an entire room. It is a picture of a man in total darkness walking along a dangerous trail. There is no moon in the sky. Darkness clings to him. His only light comes from the lantern in his hand. As he holds the lantern, it illuminates the step right in front of him. When he takes that step, what happens to the light? It goes forward one more step. The light is not bright enough to illuminate even ten yards ahead.

Ray Pritchard

We need the mighty Spirit of God to strengthen us to do the will of God, just as Jesus was strengthened by the angel in the garden of Gethsemane (Luke 22:43). You can pray all night, all day, all month, and all year for the enabling of the Holy Spirit, but your request will never be realized until you are prepared to do the will of God.

Stephen F. Olford

Detours are not just irritating interruptions that prevent us from directly reaching our destination. They may be a well-planned part of our spiritual journey. God often desires to guide us in a way that we would never choose. We want to drive on the straight, easy road that takes us directly home. God may send us on a circuitous route because He has a divine appointment or essential spiritual lessons for us and others. . . . Until our faith is made real during a detour on a dark road, we will only see God as the means of satisfying our own needs and serving our own purposes.

Sheila Cragg

God's guidance is not meant for our benefit alone but for others as well. When the Lord directs us, He has far more in mind than our personal needs. Everything that happens to us is not for or about us. . . . This is what it means to deny ourselves for the sake of Christ. We need to stop looking inward and being concerned about ourselves and start looking outward and watching for what the Lord desires us to do for His sake.

Sheila Cragg

I will guide you in the way of wisdom and lead you along straight paths.

Proverbs 4:11

Obedience is not optional. God demands and expects it. He may require things that seem foolish to us, but our task is to obey Him, not to evaluate His wisdom.

Cheryl V. Ford

The guidance He gives does not tell us what to do in any and every situation. His direction is much more helpful than that. It teaches the difference between right and wrong. By His Word, the Good Shepherd teaches His sheep the difference between the right path and the wrong path.

Philip Graham Ryken

Does God have a blueprint that includes everything in your life from the moment of your birth to the moment of your death? Is there a heavenly blueprint that shows what you're supposed to do on October 14, 2005? The answer to that question is, yes. But the only part of it you can see arrives each morning in the form of twenty-four brand-new hours, freshly delivered by United Angel Service Overnight Express. Please don't miss this point: God wants to teach us to trust Him step by step. He reveals His will one step at a time so that we will trust Him moment by moment.

Ray Pritchard

It is one thing to recognize the will of God; it is another thing to surrender to it. The passage in the Word of God that helps us understand God's will is Romans 12:1-2, where Paul links the life of surrender to the knowledge of that "good and acceptable and perfect will of God."

. . . Here is the will of God that you cannot afford to neglect, ignore, or disobey—because it is *good.* . . . A nurse broke down one Sunday morning at Calvary Baptist Church, New York City, under the power of and conviction of the Holy Spirit. After the service I sat alongside her and asked if I could be of help. She explained her problem: "I want to yield my life to God. I want Him to have everything, but I'm afraid God will take mean advantage of me." She was talking right out of her heart! Turning to Romans 12:1-2, I showed her that God's will is *good.* She celebrated a victory that Sunday morning!

Romans 12:2 also says that God's will is *acceptable.* . . . There is no place in heaven or earth more delightful or more enjoyable than the center of God's will. And whether you're serving the Lord as a missionary on some remote island, or whether you're in a very difficult home situation with belligerent parents, you can still be happy if you're in the will of God.

And Romans 12:2 says, "That you may prove what is that . . . *perfect* will of God." That word denotes an unfolding drama, not only experientially now, but eschatologically in a day to come. If you and I are in the center of God's will, He is not only going to condition and conform us to His image moment by moment, day by day, but He is going to bring us into all the fullness of His ultimate purpose in that eternal state.

Stephen F. Olford

Send forth your light and your truth, let them guide me; let them bring me to your holy mountain, to the place where you dwell.

Psalm 43:3

The conviction of the Holy Spirit is always precise: He identifies root causes of sin, and He moves the heart to specific acts of repentance and obedience. All those who trust God sufficiently to desire to obey Him, and who are patient in waiting upon Him, will find unfailingly that He gives clear guidance.

Mike Mason

But how shall we know what God wants of us? By paying attention to His Word and to our own consciences, by noting what circumstances allow, and by taking advice in order to check our own sense of the situation and the adequacy of our insight into what is right. Problems about God's will regularly come clear as they are bounced off other Christian minds. One's own inner state is important too. "If any man's will is to do [God's] will," not only will he know that Jesus and His teaching are from God (John 7:17), but he will be told if he is out of the way. "Your ears shall hear a word behind you, saying, 'This is the way, walk in it,' when you turn to the right or when you turn to the left" (Isaiah 30:21 RSV). If you are open to God, God will get through to you with the guidance you need. That is a promise!

While you are unclear as to God's will, wait if you can; if you have to act, make what you think is the best decision, and God will soon let you know if you are not on the right track.

J. I. Packer

O Father . . . I affirm Your plan for all things. I submit myself to Your will for my particular life, including the hardships You have ordained for me. . . . Keep my heart ablaze for You, dear Lord, until You take me home. In the holy name of Christ, amen.

Raymond C. Ortlund, Jr.

If we decide to enter into the abiding life and consistently seek His will through His Word, we will discover that God is eager to reveal His plan for our behavior. And God always keeps His word!

Tom Elliff

We want to know God's direction now. We want to have answers now to the problems we face. But answers usually come bit by bit. So while we wait, we are not always clear that we are getting those answers. That may be your situation right now. Some of the answers you need are still in process. You have some information, but you don't have it all. Only God has it all.

Roger C. Palms

You hold me by my right hand. You guide me with your counsel, and afterward you will take me into glory.

Psalm 73:23-24

The LORD will guide you always; he will satisfy your needs in a sun-scorched land and will strengthen your frame. You will be like a well-watered garden, like a spring whose waters never fail.

Isaiah 58:11

Therefore, since we are surrounded by such a great crowd of witnesses, let us throw off everything that hinders and the sin that so easily entangles, and let us run with perseverance the race marked out for us. Let us fix our eyes on Jesus, the author and perfecter of our faith, who for the joy set before him endured the cross, scorning its shame, and sat down at the right hand of the throne of God. Consider him who endured such opposition from sinful men, so that you will not grow weary and lose heart.

HEBREWS 12:1-3

a bright
tomorrow

Running to Win

GOD COMPELS US
TO STRENGTHEN
OUR SPIRITUAL LIFE.
THE GOAL OF ALL
SPIRITUAL TRAINING
IS TO BECOME FIT
SERVANTS OF CHRIST,
TO BECOME MORE
AND MORE LIKE HIM.

Sheila Cragg

Remember the children's story

about the race between the tortoise and the hare? This popular

tale shows that how you start out is not nearly as important as

how you finish—a truth that certainly applies to the race of the

Christian life. If the overconfident hare had stuck to the business

of running, he would have blown away his opponent. And we who

run must beware of distractions that would put us temporarily or even

permanently off course. The writer of Hebrews had the solution. We

will not stray if we fix our eyes firmly on Jesus and rely on His help

every step of the way.

Faith must go on being exercised. Faith must mean everything today, or in some tomorrow it may mean nothing. Yesterday's experiences, insights, answers to prayer, ways of putting things were completely legitimate and satisfying yesterday, but today is another day. God's truth and God's love will always be fresh, but will the same be said of our response? Will our faith and love for Him be as fresh? Paul's question to the Christians in Corinth is a question for us all: "Examine yourselves: Are you living the life of faith? Put yourselves to the test" (2 Corinthians 13:5).

Os Guinness

Nothing is more disturbing than to see Christians who have little desire to win. . . . They are content simply to be saved and to wait to go to heaven. But that's unacceptable in the Christian life.

If you claim allegiance to Jesus Christ as your Lord, you need to strive for as much excellence as you can in every endeavor. If you're a Sunday school teacher, be the most excellent teacher you can be. If you're a Bible study leader, lead your flock with excellence. If you're a homemaker, make your home as excellent as it can be. When you're at your job, do the most excellent work you can. That's the only way to live the Christian life. It takes discipline, but we must demand excellence of ourselves and run the race to win.

John MacArthur

Spiritual strength for believers is essentially an attitude of courage, and it includes such virtues as courage of conviction, courage to be uncompromising, courage to confront error and false doctrine, and courage to face intimidation and persecution and still remain true to what is right.

A strong Christian is one who lives by principle rather than whim or opinion. He doesn't always seek the easy path or safe place but faces various challenges, takes serious risks when necessary, and stands firm against opposition to the truth. He is decisive and has fixed purposes and goals, and he moves forward even if it's a painful struggle at times.

John MacArthur

God's ways of training us spiritually are not our ways; His ways of conditioning our faith are not ours. Because the way to a deeper spiritual life is often difficult, we falter at obstacles, stagger over heartaches, and stumble over hardships. . . . We may be over-loaded with guilt because of certain sins we can't overcome, and we give up and sit on the sidelines. But our Lord doesn't want us to sprint the spiritual race in shame. He wants us to run a lifelong marathon by grace—grace that cleanses us from sin, grace that frees us to run at a steady pace, grace that quenches our spiritual

thirst, sweet grace that gives us an extra surge of energy. And when we trip over hurdles, we can trust the Lord's unfailing mercy to pick us up and help us keep going on the sweaty racetrack of life.

Sheila Cragg

You need to persevere so that when you have done the will of God, you will receive what he has promised.

Hebrews 10:36

We need the support of others to run a disciplined spiritual race. If we're going to lead a godly life, we need to be accountable to the Lord and other Christians. . . . As we run this spiritual race, we need encouragers who help us keep up the pace, whose example and support inspires us to continue running even when we don't feel we can put one foot in front of the other.

Sheila Cragg

As we train ourselves to be holy, we'll trip over obstacles and fall. . . . No matter how many times we fall and injure ourselves and others, we need to get up. We must continue to correct sins that cause us to stumble, rejoin the race, and keep running.

Sheila Cragg

n likening the Christian life to a race, Paul urged us, "Run in such a way as to get the prize" (1 Corinthians 9:24). You can go to the store and get a nice jogging suit, but that doesn't make you a runner. You can go get a great-looking tennis outfit, but that doesn't keep your ball inside the baseline. You can wear a football jersey with the name and number of a star player on it, but that doesn't make you a football star.

Paul is saying, don't be satisfied simply to be part of the pack. Don't compete just for show. A winner breaks from the pack, and it's clear that Paul was intent on winning his race. The problem is, a lot of us want to walk the Christian race or jog the Christian race. But if it's a race, the idea is to run as fast as you can to get to the finish line as soon as you can.

There are two good reasons why we who know Jesus Christ as Savior ought to have as the overwhelming, dominating goal of our lives to know Christ better and to serve Him more. One reason is simply because Jesus loves us and saves us. We are on our way to heaven. We have received a transfer slip out of hell. That ought to be reason enough to serve Christ without reservation and without excuses.

The second reason . . . there is going to be a payday someday. One day God is going to reward us for how we served and loved Him. . . . Paul was saying, "I love Jesus, but I also see a prize at the end of this deal, and I want to go for it. I want to be a partaker in the victory celebration." . . . We also need to run to win.

TONY EVANS

Real success and mastery in athletics or any other area requires us to go beyond past limitations, to extend ourselves further than we ever have before, to focus on the result and break barriers that used to slow us down or even stop us. Do you see how this metaphor of a race applies to you and me? As you discipline yourself and pursue your goals with God's help, you will surge past old barriers and move ahead.

Richard L. Ganz

Growing into effective spiritual men and women is simply a matter of knowing the truth (2 Peter 3:18). We increase our understanding and gain spiritual muscle as we study the Scriptures, just as going to a health club and working out will make us stronger and give us seemingly boundless amounts of physical strength and energy.

As you mature as a spiritual youth, you will possess a vigorous and passionate drive for the truth because your theology is coming into focus. You can use the Word to discern the times and trends in our society and thereby deal with the important life issues. You will believe, know, and understand what the Bible teaches about the great redemptive truths that dominate God's Word. In that sense you'll stand on firm ground and be strong.

John MacArthur

You say, ". . . I really want to please God. But I'm a man, and, you know, there are all these things around me. The world, the flesh, and the devil are really pulling me down."

Well, there is a law called gravity that says, "What goes up must come down." But many years ago the Wright Brothers came up with an idea. They said, "If we can make something go at a certain speed with enough thrust and create an aerodynamic force, we can transcend the law of gravity."

Every time you get on an airplane, those two laws, gravity and aerodynamics, are at work. Guess which one wins? If you're still here, the law of aerodynamics must have overcome the law of gravity. Notice I said overcome, not get rid of. The law of gravity is still very much in force.

But if you'll get moving with the Holy Spirit at the right speed, the law of grace will overrule the law of sin and lift you high so you can be victorious in Christ Jesus. I want to fly; how about you?

Tony Evans

During our daily journeys, we must watch for danger zones. We must wear our spiritual armor and guard our actions and behavior. We must run swiftly from temptation, be alert to our own enticing desires that lead us onto the wide road of sin, stay on the

narrow road, the one that has been marked safe and leads to life (Matthew 7:13-14). That road is Christ Himself.

Sheila Cragg

An artist once carved a woodcut titled *The Knight, the Devil, and Death*. This work of art pictures a gallant knight riding his stallion down a narrow, lonely path in the middle of the night. Lurking alongside the path are many creatures and monsters, ready to devour the knight.

But the dangerous animals can gain no advantage over the knight as long as his eyes are singularly fixed ahead, toward his destination. His focused vision keeps him safe from harm.

The wood carving represents an important truth. As long as we keep our eyes fixed on Jesus Christ, we will not be devoured by Satan. Since the devil eagerly awaits any moment in which he can distract us from Christ and thereby cause us to sin, we must keep our eyes on Christ!

If we are to overcome Satan, we must experience a growing knowledge of Christ. And as we learn more about Christ, we discover that the devil is no match for our sovereign Lord Jesus Christ. "Thanks be to God, who gives us the victory through our Lord Jesus Christ" (1 Corinthians 15:57). Let us live as victors.

Steven J. Lawson

a bright
   tomorrow

The way one begins a new exercise program is the way to begin
our devotional life. It works best to start out slowly. Personal transformation comes through a gradual but consistent commitment to
daily exercising our faith and spiritually working through concerns with our Lord. An excess of enthusiasm and a lack of con-
sistency will only defeat and discourage us. Then we won't reach
our goal to become spiritually fit servants of God.

Sheila Cragg

Strong Christians will heed the apostle Paul's words in 1
Corinthians 9:26-27: "Therefore I run in such a way, as not without aim; I box in such a way, as not beating the air; but I buffet my
body and make it my slave, lest possibly, after I have preached to
others, I myself should be disqualified." That kind of self-discipline is a necessary part of spiritual athletics. We have to bring our
bodies into subjection so our flesh, with its evil desires, does not
dominate us and lead us into some sin that will divert us and others from the true goal of spiritual warfare. But when we honor the
Lord Jesus Christ and focus on the eternal reward that awaits all
who are faithful, that will bring out only our best efforts of spiritual service.

John MacArthur

Walking! Putting one foot in front of the other. Doing it prayer-fully, trustingly. That's what we're called to do. There's nothing flashy about that. You don't break speed records as a walker, but you can cover a lot of territory and go on for a long time.

Steady walking, trusting God as you go—that's our calling. Walk like that, and you may not get the applause of the crowd, but you will get where you are going—where God wants you to be.

Roger C. Palms

The LORD watches over you—the LORD is your shade at your right hand; the sun will not harm you by day, nor the moon by night. The LORD will keep you from all harm—he will watch over your life; the LORD will watch over your coming and going both now and forevermore.

Psalm 121:5-8

The only way we can keep running until the race is over is to rely on the Holy Spirit's strength. . . . When we cross that finish line, we'll experience an exhilarating, thrilling victory celebration that will continue throughout eternity!

Sheila Cragg

Jesus demonstrated how we're to run the spiritually disciplined race. He did nothing by Himself, and neither can we. He did everything in accordance with His Father's will, and so must we. Jesus learned obedience through suffering, and so can we. As Jesus loved and obeyed His Father, so must we.

Sheila Cragg

Direct me in the path of your commands, for there I find delight.

Psalm 119:35

Jesus did not run His race of faith for the pleasure of the experience only. Certainly our Lord experienced great pleasure in healing, comforting, encouraging, and saving people. But He didn't leave His Father's presence and heavenly glory, endure temptation and hostility by Satan, suffer blasphemy and crucifixion at the hands of his enemies, and tolerate misunderstanding and denial by His disciples for the sake of the pleasures He had while on earth. . . .

Only what awaited Him at the end of His earthly ministry could have motivated Jesus to leave and endure what He did. Two things motivated Jesus: "the joy set before Him" and sitting "down at the right hand of the throne of God." Jesus ran the race of faith

for the joy of exaltation. . . . Jesus glorified God on earth by displaying the Father's attributes and completing His Father's will.

We run for the same reason Jesus did, and we achieve victory in the same way. We run for the joy of exaltation that God promises will be ours if we glorify Him on earth. By following our Lord's example, we glorify God by allowing His attributes to shine through us and by obeying His will in everything we do. . . .

As we run the race of the Christian life and follow in the footsteps of the great men and women of faith, we can joyfully look forward to receiving the crown of righteousness, which we will cast at our Lord's feet as proof of our eternal love for Him. ·

John MacArthur

God has more in store for us than we can imagine. His boundless perfections await us. He has things just waiting beyond where we've traveled during our spiritual journeys. Sure it's great to be able to stop, look around, appreciate where we have come, and say, "God has certainly done a lot for me. Look at how far He has brought me." But God calls us to keep walking. He calls us, as Paul wrote, to "press on toward the goal to win the prize for which God has called me heavenward in Christ Jesus" (Philippians 3:14).

Richard L. Ganz

hen man goes out to his work,

to his labor until evening.

How many are your works, O LORD!

In wisdom you made them all;

the earth is full of your creatures.

PSALM   104:23-24

a bright tomorrow

Work Matters

GOD HAS A GREAT WORK FOR EVERYONE TO DO. DO IT WITH ALL YOUR MIGHT—YES, AND EVEN WITH ALL YOUR FLAWS AND ALL YOUR SINS. AND IN THE OBEDIENCE OF THIS FAITH, MAGNIFY THE GLORY OF HIS GRACE, AND DO NOT GROW WEARY IN DOING GOOD.

John Piper

How do you view your work?

A way to pay the bills? Something to be gotten through as you look forward to the evening or the weekend?

Martin Luther saw work as another form of worship. He wasn't just thinking about preaching, evangelizing, or serving in some other full-time ministry. "The maid who sweeps her kitchen is doing the will of God just as much as the monk who prays—not because she may sing a Christian hymn as she sweeps but because God likes to see clean floors. The Christian shoemaker does his Christian duty not by putting crosses on the shoes he makes but by making good shoes, because God is interested in good craftsmanship," he maintained.

When Jesus redeems our lives, He wants to redeem every aspect of life, including our work. He makes all things new—not just us but also the daily labor God has given us.

Unless we reflect the sovereignty of God in all that we do, we in life deny what we affirm in the so-called time of worship.

Timothy M. Warner

We can choose to depend on the enabling power of the Holy Spirit to renew our commitment to responsibility and excellence in our work (even when we don't feel like it, even when a halfway job would get by). When we make this choice, we deepen our relationship with the God who desires to share His happiness with us and give us His gift of satisfaction in our work—and perhaps more responsibility.

Lael F. Arrington

A whole lot of my life is spent working—giving physical or mental effort toward the production or accomplishment of some task or goal. . . . Because I am in relationship with the eternal God, my work has been aimed toward eternity.

Ellen Banks Elwell

Let us not become weary in doing good, for at the proper time we will reap a harvest if we do not give up.

Galatians 6:9

When God made Adam, the first charge He gave him was to be productive. Even in a perfect environment, Adam had a job to do. If you want to be an effective and fruitful steward, taking your Master's resources and increasing them to His glory and your benefit, you need to engage in productive work.

In order to have "something to share" (Ephesians 4:28), you have to have something left over. Paul said the way you have something left over to give is by labor. . . .

You never help people who don't want to work. Part of good stewardship is seeking opportunities to be productive instead of waiting for something to be handed to you. The problem with much of our contemporary welfare system is that it is an incentive not to work.

I am not talking about people who can't work. I am talking about people who won't work. According to Paul, if a person who refuses to work comes home saying, "I'm hungry," tell him, "Starve." That's what the Scripture says.

God made us to be productive. He made us for meaningful work and made provision for us to enjoy the fruit of our work. Instead of wondering when he's going to get a slice of a handout pie, a good steward is busy baking pies, enjoying the results, and sharing what he has with others. . . .

Work Matters

Ever since the Fall, mankind has been inventing ways to avoid honest, productive labor. Your job is a major part of your stewardship from God. Are you performing as if He were your employer? Actually, He is!

Tony Evans

We gave you this rule: "If a man will not work, he shall not eat."

2 Thessalonians 3:10

Christ, the Master, is coming soon. Opportunity slips away with each passing minute. When He returns, it will be too late to recover lost opportunity. His judgment will occur immediately, and it will result in the final, irreversible disposition of all souls alive at His appearing—both faithful and unfaithful. Now is our only time to prepare. Today is the only opportunity we are guaranteed. All the resources we have belong to the Lord. Our opportunities for sharing the Gospel, our spiritual opportunities, and all temporal blessings come from His gracious hand. If these resources were ours, we could do with them as we please. But they are His, committed to us as His stewards, and we will give account at His coming for how we have used them.

John MacArthur

Often we think of serving the Lord as a major project rather than daily discovering how we can please Him in our relationships and in our ordinary tasks.

Sheila Cragg

A friend took me out to lunch recently to share what God is doing in his life. My friend served for about ten years as an international business consultant. Along the way he worked with several multinational corporations in England, Brazil, and Italy. Right now he is "in transition," beginning his own consulting firm in the Midwest. In talking about what it meant to be a Christian in the business world, my friend made a comment that stuck in my mind: "If you are happy and productive in your current job, the only reason to take a promotion is to leverage your position for the kingdom of God."

That's a tremendous insight. Use the bigger position to impact the world for Jesus Christ. Don't just climb the ladder in order to get to the top. Realize that God has put you where you are "for such a time as this." Understand that behind every open door and every promotion stands the Lord God who rules heaven and earth. As you climb to the top, remember who put you there.

Too many Christians routinely make wrong decisions because they are too career-minded and not mission-focused. What a huge difference to see all of life as belonging to the Lord Jesus Christ!

The martyred missionary Jim Elliot said, "He is no fool who gives what he cannot keep to gain what he cannot lose." If you try to save your life, you'll lose it in the end. If you lose your life for Jesus' sake, in the end you will save it.

If you live for your career, what difference will it make ten seconds after you die? If you spend your life in the service of the kingdom of God, the road may not be easy, but 10,000 years from now you'll never regret your decision.

Do you have a career, or are you on a mission for God? The answer to that question makes all the difference in the world.

Ray Pritchard

We are created in the likeness of the Creator. . . . So we are, on a finite level, people who can create. Why does man have creativity? Why can man think of many things in his mind, and choose, and then bring forth something that other people can taste, smell, feel, hear, and see? Because man was created in the image of a Creator. Man was created that he might create.

Edith Schaeffer

*I*nclude God in your everyday. How can you do that? If you know Jesus Christ as your Savior, God can now plug you into His will, into His plan. . . . If you are going to find meaning in your work, you will only find it when you are in right relationship with God.

Otherwise, you can have the best job in the world and still be empty inside, because work in and of itself can't give you meaning [See James 4:13-17]. . . . The degree to which you integrate God into your work is the degree to which you will find meaning in what you do every day. . . .

Put another way, if you don't go to work tomorrow thinking, "I'm going to work for the Lord," then you've missed the meaning of work. The quickest way to transform a bad job is with a new attitude. And the quickest way to get a new attitude is to change bosses.

Paul says if you work for the Lord, you get your reward from Him (Colossians 3:22-24). If you're just working for "the man," the man can give you whatever reward he wants. But if you're working for the Lord, the man has to give you what the Lord tells him to give you.

This is a subtle yet significant reorientation to work. God wants you to find meaning in your work, but the thing that makes it meaningful is not the task itself, but your relationship with God in the task. Tasks can change. But even if you get a project you're not excited about, if your attitude is that you are participating with God in the project, He can change the meaninglessness of work into the meaningfulness of work.

TONY EVANS

Presenting ourselves for service means seeking the Lord's guidance regarding what He would have us do at this moment. It is the discipline of serving the Lord and other people in everything we do.

Sheila Cragg

What [Martin] Luther accomplished borders on the superhuman, and of course makes pygmies of us all. His job as professor of Bible at the University of Wittenberg was full-time work of its own. He wrote theological treatises by the score: biblical, homiletical, liturgical, educational, devotional, and political, some of which have shaped Protestant church life for centuries. All the while he was translating the whole of the Scriptures into German, a language that he helped to shape by that very translation. He carried on a voluminous correspondence, for he was constantly asked for advice and counsel. Travel, meetings, conferences, and colloquies were the order of the day. All the while he was preaching regularly to a congregation that he must have regarded as a showcase of the Reformation.

We are not Luther and could never be, no matter how hard we tried. But the point here is: Do we work . . . with rigor and diligence, or are we slothful and casual about it, as if nothing really great is at stake?

John Piper

God can give you the ability to enjoy your labor. Now that starts with your relationship to Him, but it should extend to the environment where you are expending your labor. God wants you to have a job you enjoy doing and can do well for His glory.

There's nothing worse than having to get up and go to a job you hate. Tell the truth and shame the devil. But do you know why a lot of men feel that way about their work? Because all they're doing is laying bricks instead of building cathedrals. It's a perspective problem.

The goal of work is not for you to put in your forty hours a week for forty years so you can quit and go to Florida to retire. Nor is the goal of work the accumulation of wealth so that you don't have to work anymore.

The goal of work is the joy and sense of achievement you get when you accomplish a God-given task. That's what God is after; so that's what you should be after. It would be better to make less money wanting to get up tomorrow morning than to make more money wanting to stay in bed.

Tony Evans

God has given each of us varied abilities, but it's up to us to discipline ourselves so that those abilities can become skills and to offer those skills with willing hearts.

Ellen Banks Elwell

God has arranged the universe so that productive work is designed to bring a reward. It's not always a monetary reward, although that is sometimes included too, but a reward that builds character and helps to make us the kind of people God wants us to be. . . .

When a man works, he gains a sense of dignity that nothing else can bring. . . . Another benefit of work is that it teaches responsibility. . . . Work provides a challenge and a sense of accomplishment, so that when you're finished, you can say, "That's good." . . . The most obvious reward of work is the paycheck we receive, but I saved it until last because it's not first on God's list.

Tony Evans

Can I abound in every good work? Yes, because God's grace abounds toward me (2 Corinthians 9:8). What does that mean? It means that I have been given all sufficiency to do good work. Not just partial sufficiency in some things, but all sufficiency in all things.

Roger C. Palms

May our Lord Jesus Christ himself and God our Father, who loved us and by his grace gave us eternal encouragement and good hope, encourage your hearts and strengthen you in every good deed and word.

2 Thessalonians 2:16-17

Begin to think in terms of being a producer rather than just a consumer. Remember that you are working for the Lord, not just for "the man." If the only time you work hard is when you know your boss is looking, you've got an attitude problem about your work.

Working for the Lord means working with integrity and being honest. When Zacchaeus came to Christ, he paid back the people he stole from fourfold (Luke 19:8). He became a man of integrity and honesty in his work.

And, of course, make sure you are a witness for Christ at work. People ought to know you are a Christian. I don't mean necessarily that you stop working so you can witness. I mean that both by your words and by your outstanding work habits, you give witness that you belong to Christ and that you're working for the kingdom. It should be evident to your coworkers that the hand of God is on you by what you say and what you do.

The great thing is that, as Paul said in Colossians 3:24, when you work for the Lord, you get your reward from the Lord. And no one knows how to reward like He does!

Tony Evans

I go to the Lord and pray that He will give me *His heart* and *His attitude* toward work. We know that happiness and satisfaction in our work is a reasonable expectation. And when we are distressed over dirty dishes or moaning over mounds of mending, we can come to God in prayer asking for His "good and proper" gift of satisfaction in our work, even when it seems like meaningless repetition.

Lael F. Arrington

We may not know all that God has planned, only that God doesn't waste a redeemed life. We may seem to be going nowhere; we may seem to be inconsequential. We may seem to be only occupying space. Our work may seem less important than someone else's. But that may be God's plan as He uses us for a future ongoing work that we may or may not ever see. The work of God didn't start with us; it will not end with us. We are part of a larger plan.

Roger C. Palms

None of us is perfect, but when you come to the end of your days, will you feel that you have completed your tasks well? When Jesus was nearing the end of His time on earth, He didn't have regrets; rather, He spoke with confidence about completing God's work.

Ellen Banks Elwell

You will receive power when the Holy Spirit comes on you; and you will be my witnesses in Jerusalem, and in all Judea and Samaria, and to the ends of the earth.

ACTS 1 : 8

a bright

Empowered by God

tomorrow

PAUL SAID, "BE STRONG

IN THE LORD, AND IN THE

STRENGTH OF HIS MIGHT"

(EPHESIANS 6:10). THAT IS

POSSIBLE WHEN YOU TRUST

GOD AND RELY ON THE

INFINITE POWER THAT IS

YOURS IN CHRIST.

John MacArthur

Sometimes when we compare

our lives to the biblical standards for the Christian life, we can get

discouraged. Some have given up and said, "I can't live the Christian

life." That statement is more true than they may realize. We can't live

the Christian life. Only Christ can. And He wants to live it through us.

Let go of your own self-effort and yield fully to the indwelling Christ.

He will produce in you His wonderful fruits of love, holiness, peace,

patience, and self-control.

To be Spirit-filled . . . is to have all areas of life under His direction. This is not a kind of control where we are passive and the Spirit is doing something. It is an active cooperation between our wills and the will of God. It is our response to God with faith and obedience—faith that actively appropriates the promises of God and obedience that walks "according to the Spirit" (Romans 8:1, 4; Galatians 5:25).

Timothy M. Warner

You may not have great strength, but the important thing is that every nerve, fiber, bone, and sinew in your body be given over completely to the Lord Jesus. Let Him have every ounce and every inch. It has well been said, "It doesn't take much of a man to be a Christian—just all there is of him."

. . . Remember that Paul is not talking about relying upon our own strength anyway. The secret of the whole matter is that God gives to ordinary people extraordinary power. He gave Himself *for* us in order that He might give Himself *to us* and therefore live His life *through us*. The issue is not so much our responsibility as it is our response to His ability.

Adrian Rogers

I didn't see the first *Crocodile Dundee* movie, but I remember the clip they showed when they were advertising it. Crocodile Dundee was walking down the street in New York City with his girlfriend when this guy jumps out to rob them. The thief whips out a knife and says, "Give me your money!"

The girl screams, "Be careful—he has a knife!"

You know by now that I like brothers who are cool. This brother is cool. He just smirks and says in his great accent, "That's not a knife." Homeboy reaches inside his boot and pulls out the scariest knife you've ever seen. He smiles and says, "*This* is a knife." The thief's eyes get big, and he takes off.

Why wasn't Dundee afraid? Because what would normally bring fear, a knife in your face, does not bring fear when you have something bigger and better working on the inside.

You have something bigger and better working on the inside of you, the Holy Spirit. Therefore, God does not want you to be intimidated by the world. You have the Spirit's powerful indwelling presence making you a powerful person accomplishing God's powerful kingdom program through the powerful proclamation of the Gospel.

What you need to do to unleash all this power is to pray, "Holy Spirit, I am yours. Have Your way in me. I will do what You want done in the way You want it done. I will seek to glorify Christ and build God's kingdom. Be real in me because I want all of You. I give You all of me."

Tony Evans

Our faith in Christ brings blessings not just in the past and future, but in this present life as well. It brings the oil of gladness amid the battles of life. Our justification was on the basis of Christ's finished work, and our present life is to be lived on the same basis. We have a right to lay hold upon the things of God on the basis of Christ's work on Calvary. We can do so with overwhelming confidence. Christ has paid the price. We have a living Savior. Christ has finished the work. Through His finished work there is the possibility of glorying in God amid life's struggles. . . . Through Christ Jesus our Lord, amid the rough-and-tumble, we can have strength.

Francis A. Schaeffer

We have a yielded life when we care about and live for God's opinion. . . . We joyfully recognize, whether in times of blessing or suffering, that the only safety we can know is in trusting, obeying, and surrendering our lives to the living God.

Rebecca Manley Pippert

We only become truly ourselves, and most authentically human, when we live and walk before God in complete transparency, intimacy, passionate love, and unapologetic dependence upon him. God does not want to deprive us of our humanity. On the contrary, he wants us to understand what enhances our humanity and what destroys it. The Bible says that sin—or vice—distorts and debases our humanness but that virtue heightens it.

So to live one's life on one's toes, with maturity and skill, we must possess at least three things: (1) faith in God, for it enables us to find our true self, the self God created us to be, (2) moral knowledge, for it helps us understand what destroys our humanity and what enhances it, and (3) the power of God's Spirit, for it is through the Spirit's power (and our obedience) that we are able to walk victoriously.

Rebecca Manley Pippert

With God we can do great things. On one of his canvases, the French painter Emile Ranouf has depicted an old man dressed in fisherman's garb, seated in a boat with a little girl beside him. Both the elderly man and the child have their hands on the huge oar. He is looking down fondly and admiringly upon her. Apparently he has told her that she may assist him in rowing the boat, and the child feels she is doing a great share of the task. It is easy to see, however, that his strong muscular arms are actually propelling the boat through the waves. The painting is called *A Helping Hand*.

That is a parable of what a soul can do when it depends upon God. It is God's hand that propels us through life, even through storms, and accomplishes things for Him. So we say, "Thine is the power"—all power is Yours; we are dependent upon You, God.

R. Kent Hughes

My prayer is that you and I may experience the victory, purity, and energy of the Holy Spirit, who makes Jesus real in us.

Stephen F. Olford

When I cherish feelings of self-sufficiency, drifting away from You, call me back. Renew the sweetness of felt union with You. I take You, Lord, as all my sufficiency. If I have You, I have everything worth having, whatever else I may lack. If I do not have You, I have nothing worth having, whatever else I may possess. Cut me off from my old, natural life in Adam. Unite me with Yourself by the miracle of grace, I pray, and make Your perfect obedience mine as I stand before God now and forever. In Your holy name, amen.

Raymond C. Ortlund, Jr.

*I*n my younger years I wanted to be a surgeon; I loved watching sur-
gery (an art form of the first order!). When I held citywide crusades in
Manchester, England, I often visited a well-known hospital to watch my
good friend operate. Dr. Robert Wyse was one of England's greatest
surgeons. . . . What impressed me was the team of assisting surgeons
and nurses who anticipated all his needs without a single word. When
the surgeon lifted his hand, the nurse was ready with the scalpel or
suture—or whatever else was required at that moment. Not once was
there a word between them as the operation proceeded—just total
readiness and yieldedness.

Surely this is the sense of Paul's words: "Present yourselves to God
as being alive from the dead, and your members as instruments of
righteousness to God" (Romans 6:13). When Jesus wants a hand, it is
there. When He wants a voice, it is there. This is yielding faith, living
by faith in the Son of God in such close communion that whatever God
wants is available.

STEPHEN F. OLFORD

Empowered by God

The LORD is my strength and my song; he has become my salvation. He is my God, and I will praise him, my father's God, and I will exalt him.

Exodus 15:2

God is most glorified in us when we are most satisfied in Him.

John Piper

Power from God is not something for which you have to wait. If you are a Christian, you already possess His power. You have passed from spiritual darkness into the light of God. Christians live in spiritual weakness because their eyes are not focused properly. Instead of looking at what is true, they fixate on their difficult problems.

Dr. Richard L. Ganz

Our culture puts a lot of pressure on us to be self-reliant and to "believe in ourselves." We are told we can do anything we set our minds to! While such encouragement can motivate us in a positive way, sooner or later will come [an] experience to teach us how woefully inadequate we really are. Our strength and confidence need to rest not in our imagined proud independence, but in God's real power.

Rebecca Manley Pippert

a bright
tomorrow

We constantly pray for you, that our God may count you worthy of his calling, and that by his power he may fulfill every good purpose of yours and every act prompted by your faith.

2 Thessalonians 1:11

The joy of the LORD is your strength.

Nehemiah 8:10

Be strong in the Lord and in his mighty power.

Ephesians 6:10

Prayer is part of the system of cooperation between God and man that pervades nature and life. No crop waves over the autumn field, no loaf stands on our breakfast table, no metal performs its useful service, no jewel sparkles on the brow of beauty, no coal burns in hearth or furnace, which does not witness to this dual workmanship of God and man. So in the spiritual world there must be cooperation, though on the part of man it is often limited to prayers, which may seem faint and feeble, but which touch the secret springs of deity.

F. B. Meyer

God is the source of universal, transcendent truth, against which our reason, experience, and feelings are finite and error-prone, and our proper response to Him is reverence, worship, and submission. It is the relationship between the potter and the clay (Isaiah 29) that prompts us to be in awe of God's righteous power, to lay our brokenness and failure at His feet, and to long for God to fill us up and make us whole.

Lael F. Arrington

God did not give us a spirit of timidity, but a spirit of power, of love and of self-discipline.

2 Timothy 1:7

The Lord has called every believer to serve Him with a sense of priority and integrity. Yet we don't have to rely on our own strength to do so, any more than we drew upon our power for salvation. We can be assured, along with Paul, that all the spiritual power we need to serve Christ also comes from Him: "For this purpose also I labor, striving according to His power, which mightily works in me" (Colossians 1:29).

John MacArthur

Strengthen me according to your word.

Psalms 119:28

As a Christian, you possess every spiritual resource you need to fulfill God's will for your life. You need not pray for more love, for example, because His love is already poured out in your heart through the Holy Spirit (Romans 5:5). The same is true of joy (John 15:11), peace (John 14:27), strength (Philippians 4:13), and every other resource you need. The key to spiritual progress and victory is learning to apply what you already have—not seeking more.

John MacArthur

O God of love, Your mercies have claimed me, and I have surrendered. You now call me to follow You in pouring myself out for others in a lifelong series of thousands of small gestures of love, various in form and wide in distribution. Yes, Lord, I affirm Your command. Give me now the privilege of obedience. Deliver me from big-talking, self-congratulatory good intentions that feel so good but bear no fruit, and impart to me the qualities of a real, working love. Enable what You command, O Lord, and command whatever You wish. In the holy name of Christ, amen.

Raymond C. Ortlund, Jr.

There really is no other source of power for the believer. There is none that we have in and of ourselves. When God is alive in us and working through us, we have the power to overcome all the attacks of the enemy.

Timothy M. Warner

We pray this in order that you may live a life worthy of the Lord and may please him in every way: bearing fruit in every good work, growing in the knowledge of God, being strengthened with all power according to his glorious might so that you may have great endurance and patience, and joyfully giving thanks to the Father, who has qualified you to share in the inheritance of the saints in the kingdom of light.

Colossians 1:10-12

God has given us prayer, not primarily as a method for getting things or changing circumstances, but as a means of cooperating with Him.

Tom Elliff

Jesus' commands "are not burdensome" (1 John 5:3), for in the new birth God has given us the power to perform what Jesus commands, the ability to overcome "the world" (1 John 5:4-5). Who, then, has this power to overcome the world? Those who are born again, those who have genuine faith, of course—and genuine faith is defined in terms of faith's object, namely the truth that Jesus truly is the Son of God.

D .   A .   C a r s o n

Now to him who is able to do immeasurably more than all we ask or imagine, according to his power that is at work within us, to him be glory in the church and in Christ Jesus throughout all generations, for ever and ever!

E p h e s i a n s   3 : 2 0

When we have too great a confidence in our limited knowledge, we tend to forget about God. We forget to seek Him out in prayer, through His Word, and even by way of godly counsel—all because we believe we have the answers. This is a dangerous place to be in. Since it ignores God's wisdom and denies Him His rightful place, it is the very opposite of worship.

D o n n a   M o r l e y

He said to me, "My grace is sufficient for you, for my power is made perfect in weakness." Therefore I will boast all the more gladly about my weaknesses, so that Christ's power may rest on me. That is why, for Christ's sake, I delight in weaknesses, in insults, in hardships, in persecutions, in difficulties. For when I am weak, then I am strong.

2 Corinthians 12:9-10

The Lord's will is that we gain victory over our sins by His enabling power and our humble cooperation and obedience.

Sheila Cragg

Christ lives in me. The life I live in the body, I live by faith in the Son of God, who loved me and gave himself for me.

Galatians 2:20

Christianity is primarily a life. It is a power. It is a manifestation of energy. And as we realize that the living God is among us, we shall realize more and more this tremendous power.

Martyn Lloyd-Jones

CHAPTER SIX

He who dwells in the shelter

of the Most High will rest in

the shadow of the Almighty.

PSALM   91 : 1

a bright

Holy Quietness

tomorrow

LEISURE CAN AFFORD US
TIME TO SIFT, TO REFLECT,
TO MEDITATE—TO FIGURE
OUT WHERE WE'VE COME
FROM AND WHERE WE'RE
GOING, TO APPRAISE THE
WORKS OF OUR LIVES AND
DETERMINE IF THEY WERE
VERY GOOD, GOOD, OR
AT LEAST KIND OF OKAY.

Lael F. Arrington

Be still and know that I am God"

(Psalm 46:10), the Lord invites you. To become intimately acquainted

with your Lord, you will need to take time to sit at His feet, listening

to Him speak to your soul, pouring out your heart to Him. You cannot

do this on the run or with your mind full of the day's sticky clutter.

"Come away, my beloved," he calls. Come away not just to a location,

but come away with your whole mind, your whole heart, and your

whole soul.

I can wait on God knowing that He will move; the situation will change just as the seasons change. But how necessary it is to wait on Him, to become still within my spirit—even though I may be in the midst of storms—and know that He is God. As Henri Nouwen describes in *The Way of the Heart*, being silent before God protects the inner fire, the life of the Holy Spirit within me. Coming away to sit at Jesus' feet helps me tend and keep alive the fire of love for Him. And waiting—even in difficult seasons—eventually leads to praise.

Nancie Carmichael

Our loving Shepherd desires to lead us to green meadows beside still waters so He can cleanse our diseased thoughts, heal our damaged lives, and restore our souls. He longs to guide us through the valley of pain, to free us from the fear of evil, to comfort us with His rod and staff. He yearns to lead us along the path of righteousness for His name's sake.

Sheila Cragg

Let the peace of Christ rule in your hearts, since as members of one body you were called to peace.

Colossians 3:15

Lord, I do not say, "Be with me," for of course You are! I say, "Open my eyes to Your presence." I praise You for Your faithfulness and mercies that You offer new every morning. Thank You for showing me that I do not have to generate answers—I simply must stay plugged into You, the true vine.

Nancie Carmichael

The "secret place" is not a place just to visit, but it is a place to abide, to dwell. Coming there requires being aware of where I am most afraid, most confused, most worried—and then inviting God into those places. It is humbling to be weak, but that is how God becomes strong in us. The prophet Isaiah urges us, "Come, my people, enter your chambers, and shut your doors behind you; hide yourself, as it were, for a little moment" (Isaiah 26:20 NKJV).

Nancie Carmichael

The secret place is not just a physical place; it's a place in the spirit, a place where God says, "You feel inadequate? Good. Meet Me here! I am El Shaddai." The secret place is different from time to time. But it has a similar theme—it is a place where I see my helplessness against life and throw myself on God's mercy.

Nancie Carmichael

Holy Quietness

The LORD your God is with you, he is mighty to save. He will take great delight in you, he will quiet you with his love, he will rejoice over you with singing.

Zephaniah 3:17

Has your relationship with Christ become too busy? Are you too hurried to spend time with Him? Are you too active? Too distant? Too cold? Too impersonal?

Then take decisive steps right now. Remember how it was when you first met Christ. Repent of your cold-heartedness. Repeat the basics—Bible study, fellowship, worship, and prayer. Remain on track in your fight against sin. Determine to be alone with Christ.

Have you left your first love?

He's waiting to be alone with you.

Just Him and you.

Steven J. Lawson

Those who walk in the ancient path and the good way find rest for their souls, which is exactly what people find when they come to Jesus Christ. He is the ancient, good, restful, and peaceful way.

Philip Graham Ryken

Why does the shepherd make his sheep lie down in green pastures? Because his sheep get stressed out from their unwise decisions, their battle scars, and their wanderings. They wouldn't choose to lie down and rest; the shepherd has to make them. Sound familiar?

When the Shepherd of our lives makes us lie down, He brings us to a place of complete rest and solitary quietness. It is then we can hear His voice as He walks with us, calling our name, speaking words of healing and peace. God desires to share a quiet place with us. "In repentance and rest is your salvation, in quietness and trust is your strength" (Isaiah 30:15). . . .

Serenity is found in quiet times with your Shepherd. . . . We grow most when we listen to or read God's Word, then sit back and meditate on its truth. You see, most of us are too busy or distracted to be still and meditate. Psalm 1 says [of the blessed man], "In his law doth he meditate day and night" (v. 2). . . . God is calling us to rest with Him.

ADRIAN ROGERS

It is hard for me to wait. Even microwave meals take too long to my way of thinking. Sometimes my impatience carries over into my relationship with God, but it's been said that "he who waits for God loses no time." . . . I believe we all need places to be alone with God, especially in our most challenging times of life. And our hectic and invasive times require solitude more than ever, although it's always been true that we must come away.

Nancie Carmichael

Often work, family responsibilities, and leisure activities so consume every moment that we become overly exhausted, and we miss our quiet time. Make a commitment to change your schedule.

Sheila Cragg

I meet people who don't have peace. They look for it through pleasure-seeking, therapy, new sexual relationships, alcohol, drugs. They are unhappy; they have pain, but they try to deal with it the best way they know how. Often I find myself praying for them, asking God to help them know what millions of people do know—real peace, the peace of God. That peace is not just the result of the end of wars or fighting within ourselves or with others. It is a complete peace, a perfect peace, because it is God's peace.

Roger C. Palms

Now that I travel more than I used to, I realize anew as I snuggle under my comforter that there is nothing like my own bed! Part of what relaxes me so is knowing this is my own place, and I am safe here. I don't have to impress anyone with brilliant conversation or worry about my hair. It is a place to relax, to be near the ones I love the most. . . .

Do I know what it means to enter into His rest . . . ? Understanding what Sabbath means is important—our Creator God knows our complexities, that we need times of rest and renewal.

Nancie Carmichael

Then the LORD said to Moses, "Say to the Israelites, 'You must observe my Sabbaths. This will be a sign between me and you for the generations to come, so you may know that I am the LORD, who makes you holy.'"

Exodus 31:13

God did not have to rest after creation. Regardless of how great the outflow of His power, He was not depleted one whit. But He delighted to rest, and He blessed and sanctified the seventh day— and the sabbatic pattern.

R. Kent Hughes

Every person's weekly schedule should have a day of rest from work (the Sabbath or Sunday). There should also be personal time for at least some satisfying interests for each member of the family or community. Many busy people find that if they examine their week, they spend an alarming amount of time watching TV or videos. They would discover that they feel more alive taking a walk and giving it their full attention—smelling rain on dry ground or freshly cut grass, gazing at cloud shapes, listening to and noticing birds. They would learn how satisfying it can be to read a good book or perhaps study a subject such as art or architecture with interesting (and free) books from the library or take a course. Most of us would enjoy joining a group to discuss literature or poetry or to learn a skill such as quilting, needlepoint, carpentry, or furniture restoration. Others join great and little choirs or orchestras or put on plays with local drama groups. . . . We can be poor in finances or poor in free time or energy.

Susan Schaeffer Macaulay

Our peace with God is not just some introspective thing. It is a peace based upon God's promise that Christ's atoning death is enough to meet all our present failures.

Francis A. Schaeffer

CHAPTER SEVEN

For the LORD watches over

the way of the righteous,

but the way of the wicked

will perish.

PSALM 1 : 6

a bright
tomorrow

The Way of the Godly

THE QUEST FOR HOLINESS
IS THE QUEST FOR
SATISFACTION IN GOD.
AND SATISFACTION IN
GOD IS A DIVINE GIFT OF
SOVEREIGN JOY. IT IS
SOVEREIGN BECAUSE IN ITS
FULLNESS IT TRIUMPHS
OVER ALL CONTESTANTS
FOR THE HEART.

John Piper

"Be holy because I am holy"
(1 Peter 1:16). The words blare at us from the sacred page of

Scripture. We want to run because of our pride and our fear of what

it might take to be holy. We want to be holy, but we know in our own

hearts how far we fall short. Holiness seems so awesome, so tran-

scendent, so beyond anything we can attain. But every godly person

started somewhere. So begin where you are.

It's good that we can't be holy in our own strength. We have to

depend on the Holy Spirit who lives in us to produce holiness. That's

His job. 🖌

I have mixed feelings about being godly because I know myself. I'm quick to sin and slow to be holy. All it takes is a few unguarded words, a deliberate or impulsive wrongful action, and a sinful thought, which come so naturally. Holiness is supernatural and requires that we submit ourselves to God's Word and to the Holy Spirit so that He may transform us. Godliness is a whole new way of being.

Sheila Cragg

Continual communion with God that is informed by godly attitudes, which have been shaped by godly thinking, is therefore the foundation of a Christian's useful ministry. When you are diligent to absorb God's Word daily by reading, studying, and meditating, godly responses to all the challenges of your life will become second nature. When the three dimensions of sound judgment, spiritual alertness, and prayerful communion are present and working together in your life, you'll have an overwhelming sense of God's presence and will manifest spiritual power that will influence others for Christ.

John MacArthur

To be holy, we need to release our lives to the Lord so that He may guide and instruct us in the way He desires us to go.

Sheila Cragg

What is the fruit of a life submitted to God? We become like Him! One of God's goals is to shape our character so that we will manifest His kindness, mercy, love, purity, wisdom, and so on, in ways that are reflected through our own distinctive personalities. To put it another way, God is making us holy. But there is a requirement in learning how to submit to God's authority: humility. We won't get very far in the development of holiness if we are defensive about our flaws. That is why truly holy people are so easy to be with. They have been around God too long to try to pretend they are perfect. They are the first to acknowledge their pride and their faults.

Then why are holy people so joyful and radiant? One reason is that they know that the answer to their character problem doesn't reside in them but with God. They don't try to please God through the efforts of the flesh, such as moralism or legalism, but by their obedient walk in the Spirit. They know a surrendered life comes by listening to God, walking in step with Him. . . .

Holiness comes from knowing that obedience must arise out of communion with God, who will give us everything we need. It also comes from committing our wills wholeheartedly to obeying God's commands.

REBECCA MANLEY PIPPERT

Influence is powerful, especially influence by example. Our impact on others is not something abstract but very real and active in our lives—for better or for worse. . . . Long after we have left this world, our example can influence our descendants. What example will you leave? In the worst-case scenario, we will affect future generations by our sins (Deuteronomy 5:9), or in the most blessed way, our lives will inspire those who come after us toward godliness (Deuteronomy 4:9; 6:5-7).

Donna Morley

Because we act according to the way we think (Proverbs 23:7), it's crucial to guard our minds and focus them on God and what pleases Him.

John MacArthur

I have often searched my own heart, asking myself, am I discontented with what God is fostering in my life? Do I resent it when He has to take something away or cause a delay to accomplish His purposes? Am I content to go without some things for the sake of spiritual growth? Am I more interested in holiness than in the "good life"?

Donna Morley

Since we have these promises, dear friends, let us purify ourselves from everything that contaminates body and spirit, perfecting holiness out of reverence for God.

2 Corinthians 7:1

Perfection is the goal of God's sanctifying work in us. He's not merely making us better than we are; He is conforming us to the image of His Son. As much as glorified humanity can resemble incarnate, exalted deity, we will resemble our Lord. He is making us fit to dwell in His presence forever.

John MacArthur

Therefore, I urge you, brothers, in view of God's mercy, to offer your bodies as living sacrifices, holy and pleasing to God—this is your spiritual act of worship. Do not conform any longer to the pattern of this world, but be transformed by the renewing of your mind.

Romans 12:1-2

As we follow Christ, we are to model our lives after His—to learn what He is like and reflect more and more of Him in what we do and think.

Richard L. Ganz

The Way of the Godly

As we avail ourselves of our Lord's promises and His tender, loving forgiveness, we'll experience cleansing and healing. It's only then that genuine change comes about and the spiritual renewal that He so desires for us.

Sheila Cragg

But just as he who called you is holy, so be holy in all you do.

1 Peter 1:15

By divine grace we'll grow into godly persons. As we submit ourselves to God and yield our will to His, the holiness He desires of us will gradually come. We are responsible to live holy, sanctified lives—continually dying to our sins, rising to newness of life, and being changed into God's image—yet we cannot do it without the grace of God working in us.

Sheila Cragg

To him who is able to keep you from falling and to present you before his glorious presence without fault and with great joy—to the only God our Savior be glory, majesty, power and authority, through Jesus Christ our Lord, before all ages, now and forevermore! Amen.

Jude 24-25

My heart says of you,
"Seek his face!" Your face,
LORD, I will seek.

PSALM 27:8

a bright
tomorrow

Reaching for God

RECOGNIZING THAT
THE HEART IS THE
WELLSPRING OF OUR
BEING, OUR DEEPEST
INNERMOST SELF,
WE UNDERSTAND THAT
THE ENTIRE CORE
OF WHAT WE ARE
AND ALL OUR ENERGY
MUST BE DEVOTED
TO LOVING GOD.

R. Kent Hughes

The Creator of the whole universe desires your company. He wants to talk with you. He wants you to know Him intimately. How amazing! In fact, He created you for the purpose of knowing Him. Let your soul reach out for Him.

Can you picture your heart actually moving closer and closer, more into the love of Christ? Will your heart really be happy anywhere else?

Roger C. Palms

Loving God is being so satisfied in God and so delighted in all that He is for us that His commandments cease to be burdensome.

John Piper

God is personal and therefore knowable. He is a spirit, but He has all the characteristics of personality—He thinks, feels, acts, relates to persons, and speaks to His creatures through Scripture. God wants to communicate with men and women.

John MacArthur

Great faith has very small beginnings. It begins with opening ourselves to God. When we come to Him and expose our dark hearts to the light of His grace and truth, the roots of our lives are forced down into the soil of His amazing love. Then, miraculously, just as green shoots of the mustard plant come out of the ground and grow to heights of four to fifteen feet, we see shoots of faith appearing in our lives.

Ellen Banks Elwell

When Christ comes into our lives, He does so to "dine" with us. Eating a meal pictures close fellowship with another person. It represents sitting down across the table from someone and fellowshipping with that person. Visiting. Talking. Listening. Encouraging one another. Intimate friendship.

That's what a personal relationship with Christ is like. We can pour out our hearts to Him and tell Him anything we want. We can share with Him our deepest concerns and greatest needs. What a privilege.

Have you opened your heart and received Jesus Christ? If not, why not now? You're not saved by merely knowing some intellectual facts about Christ. Nor are you saved by coming to church or doing enough good works. Salvation means inviting Jesus Christ to come live within your heart. It is experiencing a personal, life-changing relationship with Him.

Steven J. Lawson

God is a Person, and He feels, as well as thinks and acts. . . . He is our Father, when we have come to be His children, and we ought to tell our Father how much we love Him, as well as tell other people what a wonderful Father He is! You see, God really does love *people*, and He really *is* love.

Edith Schaeffer

How great is the love the Father has lavished on us, that we should be called children of God! And that is what we are!

1 John 3:1

How wonderful to realize that Jesus Christ, who is both the full expression of God and the exact reproduction of God's nature in human history, can come into our lives and give us light to see and to know God! His light is the source of our spiritual life. And His light gives us purpose, meaning, happiness, peace, joy, fellow-ship—*everything*—for all eternity.

John MacArthur

We know we have reached a spiritual turning point when we realize that our identity is found in Christ, not in other people, circumstances, or our position in life. We are more aware of God's ever-loving presence and working in our lives. We have a fresh desire for God's Word and long to know His will and seek His guidance. We know we have changed directions when we have a richer prayer life, recognize how the Lord is changing us, and are growing in faith. We're more committed to being faithful in worshiping the Lord and serving Him.

Sheila Cragg

A number of years ago our church was burglarized. Upon arriving at my office the morning after the crime, I noticed that something was amiss—the church office door was beaten to splinters, and my office door was scarred by the forceful use of a crowbar.

When the police arrived, they called for a crime scene investigator. Some clues were obvious, such as the massacred door and the trail of muddy footprints. Yet it was not these blatant clues that finally identified the perpetrators. What led the police to the burglars was virtually invisible to the naked eye—fingerprints. . . .

This common detective practice is illustrative of how the Holy Spirit leaves evidence of His activity in our lives. Sometimes the evidence is blatant, as when His deep footprints can be seen easily. Yet other times His work is more subtle, even almost invisible. But with careful examination, it is possible to discern His work from our own and to see His fingerprints on our lives.

For all of us who are children of God, these fingerprints will exist. They are the testimony of the Spirit's work in our lives. His Spirit does testify with our spirit that we are the children of God, and every believer can find enough evidence for a conviction.

DAVID HANEY

We cannot force growth. But when we choose to have a relationship with God and His body, the church, we will experience His
grace. And when we choose to read His Word and obey it, His
Spirit teaches us His truth. God's grace and truth over time always
produce growth in the believer's life.

Ellen Banks Elwell

When I consider your heavens, the work of your fingers, the moon
and the stars, which you have set in place, what is man that you
are mindful of him, the son of man that you care for him?

Psalm 8:3-4

If you were asked to give a mental picture of security, what would
it be? . . . My picture would have me running into God's arms,
knowing that He cares for me even though He has time for everyone else in the world who also wants to spend time with Him. No
matter what kind of rejection any of us has experienced, we know
that if we come to God, He will *never* forsake us. That's the ultimate in security.

Ellen Banks Elwell

Yet to all who received him, to those who believed in his name, he gave the right to become children of God.

John 1:12

Having thanked God for what you have, have you got this longing for more? Hope, faith, assurance, full assurance, enjoyment, glory. Ask Him for it. Climb the steps. Follow the example of Moses. Enter boldly in faith, and say to God, "Show me Thy glory." And you have the assurance . . . that if you do so from your heart, and sincerely, in His own good season He will answer you. You have the infinitely higher and greater assurance of this word of God itself, of the promise of the living God: "Draw nigh to God, and he will draw nigh to you" (James 4:8).

Martyn Lloyd-Jones

When I became a Christian, God came to live in me. God lives in heaven, but now He also lives in me. He lives in the deepest parts of me, and that means as I walk with Him, I can trust my deepest instincts. In fact, I must trust them, for they are the habitation of God.

Mike Mason

You have made known to me the path of life; you will fill me with joy in your presence, with eternal pleasures at your right hand.

Psalm 16:11

Knowing God doesn't come through intellectual activity—it comes as a result of our obedience to Him.

Ellen Banks Elwell

I will give you a new heart and put a new spirit in you; I will remove from you your heart of stone and give you a heart of flesh. And I will put my Spirit in you and move you to follow my decrees.

Ezekiel 36:26-27

Our greatest personal need is to know God's love. Our deepest spiritual need is to love the Lord with all our heart and all our soul and all our strength (Deuteronomy 6:5).

Sheila Cragg

Remain in me, and I will remain in you.

John 15:4

This is not an empty universe. There is Somebody at home! The Creator God can be reached as you call from any spot—in a quarry, in a jungle, in a prison, in a concentration camp, on a desert during a war, from a car you're pinned under, in a plane, sitting beside a baby's crib, in a retirement facility, in an office, in a factory. No place is out of range where the "short wave" (so to speak) does not work. . . . We are known to the infinite God who even knows the numbers of hairs on our heads. . . . We call upon the One who really is there now, and who has been and will be for eternity.

Edith Schaeffer

Seek God, seek to know God, seek to know His love, seek to be filled with this knowledge and all the fullness of God. . . . We are meant to grow in grace and in the knowledge of the Lord. We are meant to be pressing forward toward the mark, forgetting the past, desiring what He is holding out before us. . . . We say, "Ah, yes, we are working for Him." And then we leave Him alone, and we go on and on in our little activities. We ask His blessing on what we are doing, but oh how often do we seek Him, Himself! God, and the Lord Jesus Christ and the presence of the Spirit in our lives—that is true Christianity.

Martyn Lloyd-Jones

We have a deep need to experience the constant abiding presence of God. We desire closeness in human relationships, but no one can be with us at all times as God is.

He watches over us and is with us wherever we go. He sees everything we do and knows our every thought. . . . If we are Christians, His Spirit dwells within us. No one is as close to us as the Spirit of God or cares more about us. He is with us, within us, and will be with us always (Matthew 28:20).

Sheila Cragg

Where can I go from your Spirit? Where can I flee from your presence? If I go up to the heavens, you are there; if I make my bed in the depths, you are there. If I rise on the wings of the dawn, if I settle on the far side of the sea, even there your hand will guide me, your right hand will hold me fast.

Psalm 139:7-10

Seek Him, stir yourself up to call upon His name. Take hold upon Him, plead with Him as your Father, as your Maker, as your Potter, as your Guide, as your God. Plead His own promises. Cry unto Him and say, "Oh, that Thou wouldst rend the heavens, that Thou wouldst come down."

Martyn Lloyd-Jones

CHAPTER NINE

I have hidden your word in my heart that I might not sin against you.

PSALM 119:11

a bright

Spiritual Disciplines

tomorrow

TO REACH THE GOAL

OF SPIRITUAL MATURITY

REQUIRES DISCIPLINE

AND SINGLE-MINDED

OBEDIENCE.

Sheila Cragg

Do you really believe that you can become Christlike—both in character and in power to do God's work? Do you really think you can carry out Christ's commands? (Remember the Sermon on the Mount.) Are you experiencing the power that transforms ordinary sinners into extraordinary saints?

All these things are possible if we do what Jesus did while He was here among us. His whole lifestyle enabled Him to draw constantly from His Father's ample provision. What did Jesus do? He practiced spiritual disciplines such as solitude, silence, prayer, fasting, study and meditation on God's Word, service to others, and simple living.

Down through the centuries, the men and women whose names and deeds constitute the history of the church have practiced these disciplines. Great Christian leaders as well as rank and file believers have made these practices the cornerstone of their lives. Now it's your turn to carry the torch and pass it on to the next generation. Will you be found faithful?

If we need to eat regularly, we need to read the Bible regularly.

Francis Schaeffer

God's Word nourishes me, gives me courage to go on. . . . It is by being nourished by His Word that I can give out to others.

Nancie Carmichael

How sweet are your words to my taste, sweeter than honey to my mouth! I gain understanding from your precepts.

Psalm 119:103-4

Oh, how I love your law! I meditate on it all day long. God's law is the full verbalized richness of the Scriptures' explanation of the commands of God. Oh, how I love the Scriptures, the true Word of God, as I read them and think about them and come to fresh understanding day by day.

Edith Schaeffer

When you have settled that God's Word is true regardless of what the world says, your heart becomes a seed-bed for faith. And when you have faith, you are ready to pray and keep on praying.

Tom Elliff

Lt. General William K. Harrison was the most decorated soldier in the 30th Infantry Division, rated by General Eisenhower as the number one infantry division in World War II. General Harrison was the first American to enter Belgium, which he did at the head of the Allied forces. He received every decoration for valor except the Congressional Medal of Honor . . . (he was one of the few generals to be wounded in action). When the Korean War began, he served as Chief of Staff in the United Nations Command—and because of his character and self-control was ultimately President Eisenhower's choice to head the long and tedious negotiations to end the war.

General Harrison was a soldier's soldier who led a busy, ultra-kinetic life, but he was also an amazing man of the Word. When he was a twenty-year-old West Point cadet, he began reading the Old Testament through once a year and the New Testament four times. General Harrison did this until the end of his life. Even in the thick of war he maintained his commitment by catching up during the two- and three-day respites for replacement and refitting that followed battles, so that when the war ended he was right on schedule.

When, at the age of ninety, his failing eyesight no longer permitted this discipline, he had read the Old Testament seventy times and the New Testament 280 times! No wonder his godliness and wisdom were proverbial, and that the Lord used him for eighteen fruitful years to lead Officers Christian Fellowship.

General Harrison's story tells us two things. First, it is possible, even for the busiest of us, to systematically feed on God's Word. . . . Second, his life remains a demonstration of a mind programmed with God's Word. His closest associates say that every area of his life (domestic, spiritual, and professional) and each of the great problems he faced was informed by the Scriptures. People marveled at his knowledge of the Bible and the ability to bring its light to every area of life. . . .

You can never have a Christian mind without reading the Scriptures regularly because you cannot be profoundly influenced by what you do not know. If you are filled with God's Word, your life can then be informed and directed by God.

R. Kent Hughes

Grace is getting what we don't deserve and mercy is not getting what we do deserve. As we daily thank God for His mercy to us and remember all He's done for us, we are prompted to worship Him with the beauty of holy lives.

Ellen Banks Elwell

A good conscience is a tender conscience. The consciences of the godless may be so calloused that they scarcely ever act at all; but the healthy Christian conscience . . . is constantly in operation, listening for God's voice in His Word, seeking to discern His will in everything, active in self-watch and self-judgment. The healthy Christian knows his frailty and always suspects and distrusts himself, lest sin and Satan should be ensnaring him unawares; therefore he regularly grills himself before God, scrutinizing his deeds and motives and ruthlessly condemning himself when he finds within himself moral deficiency and dishonesty. . . . The healthy Christian . . . has a sense of God's presence stamped deep on his soul, trembles at it, and tests and reforms his life daily in response to it. We can begin to assess our real state in God's sight by asking ourselves how much exercise of conscience along these lines goes into our own daily living.

J. I. Packer

Many people labor under the tragic misconception that faith is simply believing that God can do anything. Of course He can! But mere acceptance of that fact is not faith in the biblical sense. Faith is acting on what God has revealed by the Spirit through His Word as His will for our behavior.

Tom Elliff

Paul said, "Let the word of Christ richly dwell within you, with all wisdom teaching and admonishing one another . . . and whatever you do in word or deed, do all in the name of the Lord Jesus" (Colossians 3:16-17). That's the essence of a biblical lifestyle and the fruit of receiving the Word in humility. May God bless you with a teachable spirit and an ever-increasing love for His truth.

John MacArthur

Do not merely listen to the word, and so deceive yourselves. Do what it says. Anyone who listens to the word but does not do what it says is like a man who looks at his face in a mirror and, after looking at himself, goes away and immediately forgets what he looks like. But the man who looks intently into the perfect law that gives freedom, and continues to do this, not forgetting what he has heard, but doing it—he will be blessed in what he does.

James 1:22-25

We are all weak in faith. But we are not saved upon the strength of our faith, but upon the object [Christ] upon whom our faith is fixed.

Francis Schaeffer

The marvelous promise of prayer is that we are never alone, never abandoned, and never unheard, even in our simplest and least eloquent cry to God. The Holy Spirit also perfectly communicates our concerns in ways that we cannot begin to comprehend.

When you are wondering whether anyone is listening, when you are doubting whether anything you say makes it past the ceiling, when words fail you and you do not even know what to say, remember the promise of Romans 8:26 and have hope ["In the same way, the Spirit helps us in our weakness. We do not know what we ought to pray for, but the Spirit himself intercedes for us with groans that words cannot express"]. . . . When we pray, heaven listens. When we pray, the Creator of the universe pays attention. The foundations of heaven shake, and the forces of God move. When we pray, the resources that formed the universe are placed on alert, and the Father, the Son, and the Holy Spirit all get involved.

DAVID HANEY

Spiritual Disciplines

Being a Christian is a blend of doctrine, experience, and practice. Head, heart, and legs are all involved. Doctrine and experience without practice would turn me into a knowledgeable spiritual paralytic; experience and practice without doctrine would leave me a restless spiritual sleepwalker. If Christ is to be formed in me, doctrine, experience, and practice must all be there together.

J. I. Packer

For some people, study is an end in itself, or perhaps a means to the end of teaching. But even though the subject matter is Scripture, for these people there is no personal commitment to living under its precepts—to ordering their marriage, their finances, their talk, their priorities, their values, by the Word of God. They do not constantly ask how the assumptions of their age and culture, assumptions that all of us pick up unawares, are challenged by Scripture. The study of Scripture, for such people, is an excellent intellectual discipline, but not a persistent call to worship; the Bible is to be mastered like a textbook, but it does not call the people of God to tremble; its truths are to be cherished, but it does not mediate the presence of God.

D. A. Carson

Put public or social worship in the place of secret prayer, and you will find . . . that your individual insight into sin, and righteousness, and judgment, on the one hand, and into Christ your righteousness and sanctification and redemption, on the other, is waning and growing dim, and as it were, generalizing itself away into mist and cold. You will find that as an individual sinner, an individual believer, you cannot minimize your solitary, secret, individual seasons of confession, petition, and praise without the results that are to be expected. Your spiritual life-pulse will be feebler. Your whole renewed nature and its work will suffer from the center.

H. C. G. Moule

How can a young man keep his way pure? By living according to your word.

Psalm 119:9

For us as Christians, it's not likely that we . . . will be persuaded logically that the Bible is a lie and our faith worthless. It's much more likely that Satan will derail us spiritually and invalidate our message and potential to minister to others by seducing us morally. . . . "Above all else, guard your heart, for it is the wellspring of life" (Proverbs 4:23).

Lael F. Arrington

If you remain in me and my words remain in you, ask whatever you wish, and it will be given you.

John 15:7

Prayer need not always be upbeat and optimistic. The true believer does not always rise from his knees full of encouragement and fresh hope. There are times when one may remain down in the dumps and yet still have prayed well. For what God wants from us is not the observance of religious protocol, but just that we be real with Him. What He wants is our heart.

Mike Mason

Jesus asks us to apply His teaching in the everyday, in the ordinary. "If you love me, you will obey what I command."

Susan Schaeffer Macaulay

You need not be afraid to enjoy God. The beautiful thing is that He uses us, but never in the way a soldier would use a gun only to throw it down and take another. He uses us, but He always *fulfills* us at the same time.

Francis Schaeffer

or God did not give us a
spirit of timidity, but a spirit
of power, of love and of
self-discipline.

2   T I M O T H Y   1 : 7

a bright tomorrow

Help for Times of Trouble

NO MATTER WHAT HARDSHIPS WE EXPERIENCE, GOD LOVES US. HE HAS NOT FORSAKEN US AND HE WILL NOT.

Sheila Cragg

Don't be surprised when hard times overtake you, the apostle Peter warns (1 Peter 4:12). Trials for the believer are not strange; they are normal. We only grow into Christlikeness when we are stretched. God loves us too much to allow us to remain spiritual infants forever. And He is with us in every difficulty to offer a helping hand.

We may wish God had launched us down Lazy River, but it's here on Thunder River that He plans an adventure to strengthen our faith and grow our character. The wettest, wildest amusement park thrill rides pale in comparison.

Lael F. Arrington

Conflict is inescapable, but some handle it better than others. Individuals who maintain a calm disposition in the midst of difficult circumstances shine like bright stars against the dark horizon of chaos and confusion. Who are these people? They are those who find strength for their conflicts in quiet times of Bible reading and prayer.

Tom Elliff

When you and I live out who God has called us to be, our transformation will be so revolutionary that not only will we change, but we'll effect positive changes in others. We will love, give, speak kindly, be gracious, and forgive. This is part of what it means to be empowered by Christ. We will also come to realize that no matter how challenging our situations may be, not only can they work for good in us, but they can work for good in other people.

Richard L. Ganz

Why does Christ ask us to come to Him when we're discouraged and overburdened rather than when we're rested? He invites us to come because He desires to refresh us spiritually. He desires to replenish and restore our faith.

He longs to give us relief from our physical, mental, and emotional pain. He longs to give us respite from unrelenting heartaches that exhaust us and allow us no reprieve. . . . Christ calls us to come to Him when we're tired so He can give us rest from difficult human relationships and responsibilities, so He can relieve us of the burdens we bear, so He can refresh us when we're weary of the daily work we must do.

Sheila Cragg

One of our greatest fears is that we suffer for no reason, and that if we are incapacitated, we will have no value to others. Our society has devalued life and in doing so has devalued suffering. To most people pain is pointless and has no meaning other than being an inconvenience that must be done away with.

The truth we must hold on to is that the sacrifices we make in affliction and the way we trust the Lord have great significance in His eyes. . . . God loves and values us.

Sheila Cragg

How can the Lord expect me to do His will in the midst of suffering? . . . "I can do all things through Christ who strengthens me" (Philippians 4:13).

Sheila Cragg

When I encounter problems and difficulties in my life, too often my initial approach is to work hard at being strong. I like to see myself as a person who is strong physically, mentally, and spiritually. But I have discovered that even the best of my strength is no match for many of the challenges of my life on this earth. . . . God can use us when we realize we're not strong on our own and admit our weakness before Him, asking Him to take our frail offerings and use them to increase His kingdom, not ours.

Ellen Banks Elwell

Through our problems God is making available to us blessings for which we have not asked. He is allowing us to face difficulties so we will ask for and accept what He wants us to have for our welfare and His glory.

Tom Elliff

a bright
tomorrow

It seems to me that there is a need for us to be aware of our suffering giving us a tiny measure of understanding of Christ's suffering. Our prayer as we are suffering the agony of a broken shoulder, pulled ligaments, hostage captivity, postoperative pain, and so on, is to be one of thanksgiving that Christ suffered all this and so much more for us. Then we are to turn and ask for help, His strength in our miserable weakness to endure what we need to be enduring with patience (not ours but His) and to be, as well as to do, that which no one else could be. Of course we are allowed to ask for deliverance from this "round of battle," but so often we are wasting an opportunity to do and be that which we could not do or be in any other set of circumstances. There is an opportunity for learning more reality, not only the reality of Christ's suffering, but the reality of His strength in this particular set of weaknesses, His comfort in this particular sorrow of separation or pain.

EDITH SCHAEFFER

I've found that each new area of life offers opportunities to be afraid. Psalm 94:19 says, "In the multitude of my anxieties within me, Your comforts delight my soul." That's exactly what anxieties can become if left unchecked—multitudes. Fear is creative, and given free rein, it grows. Yet each new area of life, each new place offers opportunities to see with eyes of faith rather than of fear. The way out of fear, I believe, is learning the discipline of having a grateful heart.

Nancie Carmichael

If you're going through a time of suffering for righteousness' sake, take heart—the Lord went through it too, and He understands how difficult it can be. He knows your heart and will minister His super-abounding grace to you. Rejoice that you are worthy of suffering for Him and that the kingdom of heaven is yours.

John MacArthur

If when trials beset you, you tend to think you are alone and singled out for trouble, remember you have company. You stand in a long line of pilgrims stretching down through the ages whom the Lord has told, "Be strong; take courage; I am with you."

Cheryl V. Ford

He knows everything that happens to us, both good and evil. Surely, the Lord our Shepherd is guiding us through the darkest valleys, deepest rivers, and fiery trials. His thoughts of us are precious and so constant we cannot count them, for they number far more than all the grains of sand in the world (Psalm 139; Isaiah 43:2). What great comfort to know that God is constantly watching over us and listening to us.

Sheila Cragg

To be surrounded by God's hedge . . . does not always mean to be protected from evil and from all the shocks of life. The hedge may be a hedge of thorns, and often enough the loving protection of the Lord involves being thrust into the very midst of evil, and being asked to carry this burden up the hill to Calvary. Whatever our circumstances, the safest place to be is always in the Lord's will. The safest place is the hollow of His hand—even (and especially) when that hollow takes the form of a bleeding nail print.

Mike Mason

If you falter in times of trouble, how small is your strength!

Proverbs 24:10

Even severe trials needn't rob you of your joy. James 1:2 says you should be joyful when you encounter various trials because trials produce spiritual endurance and maturity. They also prove that your faith is genuine, and a proven faith is the source of great joy (1 Peter 1:6-8).

John MacArthur

Do not let your hearts be troubled. Trust in God; trust also in me.

John 14:1

Are trials pressing you hard today? Lift your eyes from your circumstances and look into the face of God. He is waiting for you to come to Him for help. Think upon the glorious inheritance He is keeping for you in heaven if you persevere to the end.

Cheryl V. Ford

Through our problems God is reminding us that we are still in His school of prayer. The Scriptures tell us repeatedly that God's provision comes in answer to petition and intercession. The needs of our lives today are part of God's plan to keep us praying.

Tom Elliff

God is already at work to restore the world and to redeem us. He is not away or asleep or unaware or unconcerned. No—He is at work. In fact, when we see the harsh realities of this world, we can be encouraged, for we know that all the tragedy and the suffering will not equal all that will one day be revealed in, by, for, and to us.

David Haney

Is any one of you in trouble? He should pray. . . . The prayer of a righteous man is powerful and effective.

James 5:13, 16

Our problems are a call to worship. That was Job's immediate response to all that befell him. Is it ours? We each would do well to make a list of our needs, and then let the world and the devil see how powerful God is as we attach new meanings to our troubles and praise our awesome God in every situation, no matter how troubling or taxing.

Tom Elliff

As always with God, He gives us the better end of the deal. We give Him our worries, our requests, and our thanks, and He gives us His peace.

Ellen Banks Elwell

You, dear children, are from God and have overcome them, because the one who is in you is greater than the one who is in the world.

1 John 4:4

Praise be to the God and Father of our Lord Jesus Christ, the Father of compassion and the God of all comfort, who comforts us in all our troubles, so that we can comfort those in any trouble with the comfort we ourselves have received from God.

2 Corinthians 1:3-4

Many a Christian has experienced the almost ineffable release of being transported from despair or illness or catastrophic defeat or a sense of alienated distance from God, to a height of safety or health or victory or spiritual intimacy with our Maker and Redeemer. . . . The apostle Paul can speak of "our light and momentary troubles" (though by our comfortable Western standards his troubles were neither light nor momentary!). These achieve for us "an eternal glory that far outweighs them all" (2 Corinthians 4:17)—and on such a scale they truly are light and momentary.

D. A. Carson

a bright
tomorrow

It is when we are suffering and forgotten that God often unexpectedly breaks into our lives to use us in the greatest ways.

Steven J. Lawson

I have often said that I am thankful for those times when all props were knocked out from under me, not because I enjoy the fear, confusion, and pain, but because those . . . are the times when I know most assuredly that "God is our refuge and strength, an ever-present help in trouble. Therefore we will not fear, though the earth give way and the mountains fall into the heart of the sea, though its waters roar and foam and the mountains quake with their surging" (Psalm 46:1-3). Hope shows that there is a way out.

Susan Hunt

Let me walk through life seeing Your power above and beyond the doubtful circumstances, the uncertainties, and the crises around me and within me. Let me, O God, live by true faith, enabling me especially to obey Your hard commands. In the holy name of Christ, amen.

Raymond C. Ortlund, Jr.

Do not let your hearts be troubled and do not be afraid.

John 14:27

The LORD is close to the brokenhearted and saves those who are crushed in spirit. A righteous man may have many troubles, but the LORD delivers him from them all.

Psalm 34:18-19

Are you happy with the way God is shaping your life? God often makes something out of us that we do not have in mind. We have disappointments in love. We have diseases in our bodies. We have discouragements in our work. We have desperations in our families. For one reason or another, we are often unhappy with the way life is shaping up. Very likely, if you were behind the potter's wheel, you would make you differently. . . .

You are not the Potter. You are only clay. The proper thing for clay to do is trust the Potter and yield to His hands. . . . Are you willing to trust the Potter? Do you believe that He knows best, shapes best, fashions best? If you have given your heart to God, you can trust Him to transform you into something useful and beautiful. If that seems hard to believe, it is because He is not even close to being finished yet. He is taking the time to work on the parts of your life that are still lumpy and off-center. Some parts He may need to smash down and raise up all over again. Will you trust Him—really trust Him—to do what is best?

Philip Graham Ryken

O triumphant Man of Sorrows, why am I so afraid of suffering? Have I forgotten that You draw near to Your sufferers with special manifestations of Your mercies, more than compensating for the adversity? Have I forgotten that You convict the world through a suffering, not a triumphant, church? Have I forgotten that it is not by might, nor by power, but by Your Spirit? That when I am weak I am strong? That Your grace is made perfect in my weakness? That the willing loss of earthly things for the sake of heavenly things is a powerful witness to the reality of those unseen treasures before a world enslaved to the tangible? Lord, I am no hero. I only want to live a quiet life with my family and be left alone to get on with my ministry. But the world is becoming increasingly hostile to Your claims. And I am learning that, if You do ordain that I should seal my testimony to You with suffering, I have nothing to fear. You will be there for me. You will be there at my side. You will not let my faith die and discredit You. Nothing can wrench me out of Your loving embrace. I now receive, and I treasure, Your assurance and peace. In Your holy name, amen.

Raymond C. Ortlund, Jr.

Take your sufferings to that secret place where you meet God in prayer. That is where you must take them. Where else can you unburden your heart so freely? Who else will comfort you so tenderly? There is no need to hide your troubles. Take them to the Lord in prayer.

Philip Graham Ryken

I know that genuine hope can prevail in any struggle. I know that God is weaving the fabric of our lives with a purpose, even when the threads seem tangled to the point of ruin. I know that this kind of hope is available to anyone who wants it.

But I also know this hope requires affirmation and validation. For our hope to remain strong, we must cultivate it, nurture it, and spread it around. We must draw from the well of God's Word and drink often, lest our hope dry up. We must exercise our hope, lest it atrophy and grow weak. And we must remember that the Source of our hope is always available and ever eager to replenish our supply.

David Haney

Much of the work of faith consists in this: In bad times to remember the good, and in good times to remember the bad. Practicing the former gives birth to hope; practicing the latter aborts pride.

Mike Mason

CHAPTER ELEVEN

Blessed is the man who fears
the LORD, who finds great delight
in his commands. His children will
be mighty in the land; the generation
of the upright will be blessed. Wealth
and riches are in his house, and his
righteousness endures forever.

PSALM 112:1-3

a bright

Are You a Success?

tomorrow

I HAVE LEARNED TO
RECOGNIZE AND
CELEBRATE MY GIFTS,
TO ENJOY MY CALLING,
TO REVEL IN MY UNIQUE
PLACE IN GOD'S PLAN.
THERE IS GENUINE
SATISFACTION IN WHO
I AM, WHAT I HAVE,
WHERE I'M GOING,
AND WHAT I CAN
GIVE TO OTHERS.
IT IS ENOUGH.

Roger C. Palms

What is the true measure

of success? The world has one view; God's Word has quite another. It's

a great temptation to have and do what is acceptable in our fallen cul-

ture. All Christians face the pressure to seek the praise and admiration

of others, the "good things" in life, career achievement, and other goals

the world deems essential. If we choose godly values and a godly

lifestyle, many will criticize or laugh or write us off as losers. But on

that final day when we stand before the Lord to account for our lives,

those people's opinions will not matter. Only God's smile of approval

will mean anything to us then.

O Lord, I used to cherish the most exquisite sense that I was better than most people. It felt so good, perceiving myself that way. It felt good, looking down on the immortal masses from a position of superiority. I even looked down on other Christians who failed to meet my particular standards of acceptability. That feeling of superior virtue was delicious, but it was also self-deceived. I repudiate it, Lord. I pour contempt on it, for it demeans You. It demeans Your cross. Now I embrace You alone as my *only* legitimacy before God. You alone are my wisdom, righteousness, sanctification, and redemption. You alone are my narrow escape. Now, when I boast, let me boast only of all that You are to me. In Your holy name, amen.

Raymond C. Ortlund, Jr.

Watch how often people, Christian people, become unprincipled, silly, easily manipulated, when they are in the presence of what they judge to be greatness. One of the great virtues of genuine holiness, a virtue immaculately reflected in the Lord Jesus, is the ability to interact the same way with rich and poor alike, with strong and weak alike. Beware of those who fawn over wealth and power and boast about the powerful people they know.

D. A. Carson

In Jeremiah 9:23 God says, "Let not a wise man boast of his wisdom, and let not the mighty man boast of his might, let not a rich man boast of his riches."

God says, "There is something in life worth bragging about, but it's not your bank account, your position in the marketplace, or your educational degrees." God says there is only one thing in life worth bragging about: "Do you know Me?"

It's amazing how we brag about everything else. Some of us can brag about our educational achievements. We've gone through school, and we graduated magna cum laude. . . . People treat us respectfully; they give us titles to recognize our achievement, and if we are not careful, we might boast about that.

Or you may have started at the bottom of your company, and now you're in the executive suite. Now there's extra money in the account. The home is nice. The cars are new. The clothes are authentic. All of the data necessary to indicate success might tempt you to brag.

But God says, "If you really want something to shout about, can you brag that you know Me? Because if you can't talk about that, then it doesn't matter how much money is in your account, what degrees are on your wall, or what position you have in the company."

Pride is like growing a beard. It needs to be clipped daily. Every day you and I need to get up and look at our degrees, our careers, our money, and then say, "If it were not for the grace of God . . ." See, the knowledge of God affects everything about you. God says, "If you are going to brag, brag that you know Me."

Tony Evans

If a group of men do not approve of where I am and what I do, does it prove I've missed success? No; only one thing will determine that—whether this day I'm where the Lord of lords and King of kings wants me to be.

Francis Schaeffer

I have a friend who calls occasionally to ask if the Lord has shown me "some new thing." On one occasion I replied, "I've learned how to get all I want!" He responded in surprise, "That sounds rather crass." "I know it does," I responded, "but it's true nonetheless."

Here is the truth I shared with him: If I could just get to the place in my life where all I wanted was whatever God wanted for me, then I would have all I wanted, and He would have all of me that He wanted!

Tom Elliff

The heart of much sin is the smug self-sufficiency that boasts in its own wisdom or strength or wealth. . . . That is always a mark of lostness. It focuses on self. Worse, it fails to recognize that all that we have (and boast about) is derived: We do not choose our own genes, or parents, or heritage; all we have achieved has been in function of others, of health, of gifts, of support, of situation— a thousand elements over which we have little control and which, this side of the Fall, we do not have the right to claim. Worst of all, smug and self-sufficient people leave no place for priorities outside themselves; they leave no place for God, for they are their own gods.

D . A . Carson

The humility that stops our self-centered chatter so that we can listen costs us something. How we love to prance into the limelight and live there! This is the opposite of biblical humility. . . . It turns out that it is the humble, dutiful person who finds uncluttered joy in giving full attention to life's demands. Proper foundations enable a creative, satisfying, and interesting personal life.

Susan Schaeffer Macaulay

Blessings crown the head of the righteous.

Proverbs 10:6

Millions of people buy into the false idea . . . that their happiness is God's supreme goal for them. That sounds good, doesn't it? "God wants me to be happy." "God wants me to be fulfilled." "God wants me to be successful." That thinking is used to justify all kinds of bizarre and even evil behavior. Some Christian men have said, "It is God's will that I should divorce my wife and marry another woman because we are in love, and God wants us to be happy." The correct theological term for that is, "Baloney."

If your personal happiness is not God's highest goal for you, then what is . . . ? It is God's will for you to be holy. It is God's will for you to be like Jesus Christ. It is God's will for you to be in a place of maximum usefulness for the kingdom of God.

Ray Pritchard

Do not be paralyzed by your weaknesses and flaws. Oh, how many times we are tempted to lick our wounded pride and shrink from some good work because of the wounds of criticism—especially when the criticism is true! A sense of being weak and flawed can paralyze the will and take away all passion for a worthy cause. . . . God never yet used a flawless man, save one. Nor will He ever, until Jesus comes again.

John Piper

A young violinist was giving a concert one day in front of a large crowd. He ended his concert with a flourish, and all the people stood up and applauded, shouting, "Bravo! Bravo! What a performance!" But the young man put his head down. As the people continued to clap, his eyes began to fill with tears. There was no smile on his face.

All of a sudden as the applause began to die, an old man sitting up in the balcony stood up and began to clap. As soon as the violinist saw that, a smile came across his face. He wiped the tears from his eyes. He smiled and held up his violin and walked off the stage.

A man in the wings said, "How come you were sad when the people stood up, but when that old man stood up, you became glad again?"

"Because the old man was my violin teacher," the young musician explained, "and unless he stood up, my concert would have been a failure, because he is the only one who knows . . . exactly how each piece is supposed to be played. It does not matter whether the people stand and applaud. . . ."

My friend, unless God is standing and applauding, we really haven't done anything. Don't be fooled by people's applause. Make sure that Jesus Christ says, "Well done, good and faithful servant."

TONY EVANS

Do not let this Book of the Law depart from your mouth; meditate on it day and night, so that you may be careful to do everything written in it. Then you will be prosperous and successful.

Joshua 1:8

As a human being, you are a creature of purpose, and you would describe your life in terms of goals you have had, and of challenges, conflicts, frustrations, and progress in pursuit of them.

The secular, man-centered way of doing this is by estimating achievement and non-achievement, success and failure in tasks tackled. Memoirs and biographies of public figures review their careers in this way. Bible writers, Bible characters, and biblical Christians, however, do differently.

To start with, they look at their lives God-centeredly. They see God as the one whose action has been the decisive factor shaping their lives, and as the only one who is able to assess what they have achieved.

J. I. Packer

O LORD, save us; O LORD, grant us success.

Psalm 118:25

When I was young, British, and pagan, I thought the sky was the limit, and nothing I wanted to do was beyond me. My dreams ranged from being a star cricketer to a distinguished locomotive engineer to a top comedian, with much bizarre stuff in between. But spectacular success was always part of the dream, and every failure hurt because it punctured my conceit.

When I became a Christian, which happened at university, I had the simplistic zeal you expect of a convert. . . . For years I went on thinking that spectacular success in one's work for God was the right thing to pray for, and the only sure sign that one was serving the Lord as one should. Most of my conceit, I fear, was still there. . . .

The passion for success constantly becomes a spiritual problem—really, a lapse into idolatry—in the lives of God's servants today. To want to succeed in things that matter is of course natural, and not wrong in itself, but to feel that one must at all costs be able to project oneself to others as a success is an almost demonized state of mind, from which deliverance is needed. . . . This success syndrome is an infection that has spread right through the whole Western world, so that its prevalence among Christian people, though distressing, is hardly surprising. The world's idea that everyone, from childhood up, should be able to succeed at all times in measurable ways, and that it is a great disgrace not to, hangs over the Christian community like a pall of acrid smoke. . . . Those who want to become, and in some cases be hired as, Christ's agents in building His church now feel they have to have track records that show them as successes in everything to which they ever put their hand. . . . Successful-looking performance at all costs becomes the goal, and unreality creeps into people's view of themselves as a result. . . .

The truth is that our success in the real business of church-building—not in the production of plant and programs, but the shepherd's work of gathering, nurturing, feeding, and guiding those who Christ pictures as the sheep of His flock—is something that only God is ever in a position to measure.

J. I. Packer

God's servants do not have the same gifts, the same tasks, the same success, or the same degree of divine intervention. It is partly a matter of gifts and calling; it is partly a matter of where we fit into God's unfolding redemptive purposes. . . . Let God be God; let all His servants be faithful.

D. A. Carson

CHAPTER TWELVE

*W*hoever wants to be great among you must be your servant.

MATTHEW 20:26

a bright

A Great Servant

tomorrow

OUR HEARTACHES

ARE NOT FOR US ALONE

BUT FOR OTHERS AS WELL.

THE LORD DESIRES TO USE

US TO COMFORT AND

STRENGTHEN OTHERS

EVEN AS WE SUFFER.

Sheila Cragg

Jesus set the example. He took a towel and a basin, knelt down, and washed His disciples' feet. The disciples sensed the incongruity in this act. They had seen their Master do miracles—walk on water, raise the dead. They had heard the crowds who wanted to make Him their king. They had seen the Jews try to stone Him because He claimed to be God. They were shocked that Jesus should stoop to do the task of a servant.

This act turned the disciples' entire conception of leadership upside down. His next words brought the lesson home: "Now that I, your Lord and Teacher, have washed your feet, you also should wash one another's feet. I have set you an example that you should do as I have done for you."

Jesus tells us as He told His first followers, "Now that you know these things, you will be blessed if you do them" (John 13:14-15, 17).

Peter is a good illustration of how God builds a spiritual leader. He begins with a person's natural traits and works from there. Natural traits alone don't make a spiritual leader; the person must also be gifted and called by the Holy Spirit to lead in the church and to be a model of spiritual virtue. But often God endows future leaders with natural abilities that constitute the raw materials from which He builds spiritual ministries. That was certainly the case with Peter, who demonstrated the leadership qualities of inquisitiveness, initiative, and involvement. . . .

How about you? Are you inquisitive about God's truth? Do you take the initiative to learn about Him? Do you want to be involved in what He is doing? If so, you have the raw material for spiritual leadership. Continue to cultivate those qualities, allowing the Spirit to use you for God's glory.

John MacArthur

Encourage the young men to be self-controlled. In everything set them an example by doing what is good. In your teaching show integrity, seriousness and soundness of speech that cannot be condemned, so that those who oppose you may be ashamed because they have nothing bad to say about us.

Titus 2:6-8

a bright
tomorrow

Whether you've been a Christian for many years or just a short time, you are an example to someone. People hear what you say and observe how you live. They look for a glimpse of Christ in your life. What do they see? How would they do spiritually if they followed your example?

John MacArthur

Be shepherds of God's flock that is under your care, serving as overseers—not because you must, but because you are willing, as God wants you to be; not greedy for money, but eager to serve; not lording it over those entrusted to you, but being examples to the flock. And when the Chief Shepherd appears, you will receive the crown of glory that will never fade away.

1 Peter 5:2-4

One of the most striking evidences of sinful human nature lies in the universal propensity for downward drift. In other words, it takes thought, resolve, energy, and effort to bring about reform. In the grace of God, sometimes human beings display such virtues. . . . Genuine reformation and revival have never occurred in the church apart from leaders for whom devotion to God is of paramount importance.

D. A. Carson

A Great Servant

A man willing to sacrifice all for the cause of Christ will prove eminently useful. Paul noted Timothy's availability when he told the Philippians, "I hope to send him immediately, as soon as I see how things go with me" (2:23). That was Timothy, always available, always willing to be used. At no time in the New Testament accounts did he ever appear to have his own agenda. He was always willing to serve whenever and wherever he was needed. . . .

Are you willing, like Timothy, to sacrifice your hopes, your dreams, and your plans for your Master? Are you willing to accept His nobler plans?

John MacArthur

If you gather up all the ingredients for bread, toss them into a pan, and put the pan into a heated oven, you won't get bread. The recipe says all the ingredients must be thoroughly mixed before you stick them in the oven. In similar fashion, you can't generate integrity unless you wisely apply (or mix) all the principles of God's Word into all aspects of your life. Nothing about us should be unrelated to biblical truth. We should have no cracks between the areas of our lives, no impurities in the ingredients, for they would make us less than completely genuine.

John MacArthur

There never seem to be enough leaders to go around. Leaders can't take a community any higher morally or ethically than they've been themselves, just as a pastor can't take a church higher spiritually than he's gone himself. That's why studying the life and accomplishments of Nehemiah is like a breath of fresh air. . . . [It's] the portrait of a godly leader. . . .

Nehemiah set a great example for his people. He looked over his twelve-year governorship and concluded that he had honored his God. Notice what he did and did not do.

First, unlike his predecessors, Nehemiah did not allow power or wealth to corrupt him, because he feared the Lord. That tells me you can be a Christian politician. You can serve in the government and still fear the Lord. You can be in business, law, medicine, and fear the Lord. You can be anything and honor God.

Nehemiah knew that power and wealth can corrupt. So rather than lounging in the governor's mansion and enjoying all the "perks" of office, he set himself to work on the wall of Jerusalem. He did not tell other folk to do what he was not willing to do. He led by example. We need leaders today who set the example. I don't mean being perfect, but making the effort to do it right and being open to correction when they fail.

TONY EVANS

A Great Servant

The best way to maintain integrity and avoid compromise is to keep your eyes focused on Christ. Allow Him free access to rule and guide your way through the world's toughest storms.

John MacArthur

The Lord's servant must not quarrel; instead, he must be kind to everyone, able to teach, not resentful. Those who oppose him he must gently instruct, in the hope that God will grant them repentance leading them to a knowledge of the truth.

2 Timothy 2:24-25

Sometimes God must lead you downhill to take you uphill. He must take you to the bottom in order to get you to the top. The problem comes when we're at the bottom, because we tend to assume that it's the end of the trip. But when the Lord is with you, something is going to happen. . . .

Even if you don't understand why certain things happened, God will always work out His purposes if you'll give Him a chance.

But you say, "My life is a lemon." Oh, but God can make lemonade. He can take a messed-up scenario and totally transform it if His sovereignty is allowed to work in your life.

Tony Evans

Remember, God will take the raw material of your life and will expose you to the experiences and teachings that will shape you into the servant He wants you to be. Trust Him to complete what He has begun in you, and commit each day to the goal of becoming a more qualified and effective disciple.

John MacArthur

Life is relationships: with God, men, and things. Get your relationships right, and life is a joy, but it is a burden otherwise. . . . True joy comes only through meaningful relations with God, in tasting His love and walking Christ's way. This is the real *dolce vita,* the life that is genuinely sweet and good.

J. I. Packer

When at last I begin to see that God acts in my best interest, even in life's toughest times, it doesn't focus my attention inward; it focuses my attention outward. I have so much more to give to other people when I focus outward. I can live with an abandonment that is unknown to self-centered people. You can too.

Roger C. Palms

[God] wants us to live before Him in such a way that we anticipate His promises even when every circumstance is going opposite to what those promises say. . . . If you're still anticipating
something you are asking God to do in your life, don't try to
manipulate Him or your circumstances. Let Him bring it about—
and be prepared to keep trusting Him if it doesn't happen.

Tony Evans

Whoever and whatever we are, however we are placed and wherever we serve, it will mean at least the following: attention to the
Scriptures in order to find God's will; appropriation of God in
covenant as "my God" . . . ; devotion in the form of prayers of petition, celebration, sometimes desperation, and perhaps even
imprecation when we find ourselves up against evil; preparation
to deal with . . . triumph or disaster, both of which are going to
invade our lives from time to time; expectation of help and deliverance in answer to prayer; motivation to seek God's glory by practicing full-scale obedience to Him; and a passion for the kind of
stubborn faithfulness that is resolved to honor God and show forth
His praise through thick and thin.

J . I . Packer

CHAPTER THIRTEEN

*Jesus Christ is the same
yesterday and today and forever.*

HEBREWS 13:8

a bright

On to the Future

tomorrow

HAS IT EVER OCCURRED TO

YOU THAT NOTHING EVER

OCCURS TO GOD? GOD

KNOWS ALL THINGS,

INCLUDING THE FUTURE.

Philip Graham Ryken

Just as school prepares us for life, life prepares us for eternity. The choices we make affect us not only in this world, but also in the next. Let's give much attention to the treasures we are laying up in our Father's heavenly house where we will be with Him forever. Remember, all earthly things will pass away, but what's done for Christ will last for all eternity.

God saved us so that we can one day be with Him forever in heaven. But He also saved us in order that "we may walk in newness of life" (Romans 6:4), in order that "we should bring forth fruit unto God" (Romans 7:4), and in order that "the righteous demands of the law might be fulfilled in us" (Romans 8:4). We can do all these things, not in our own power, but through Christ and His indwelling Spirit.

Francis A. Schaeffer

All for Jesus, All for Jesus! All my being's ransomed pow'rs:
All my thoughts and words and doings,
All my days and all my hours.

Mary D. James

There is no part of us that has not been bought outright. Christ alone owns our eyes to view His world. He alone owns our hands to serve His will. He alone owns our feet to walk His way. He alone owns our minds to think His thoughts. He alone owns our hearts to love Him fervently. He alone owns our personalities to radiate His charm and glory.

Stephen F. Olford

The truth of our Lord's imminent coming should motivate us to be godly, watchful pursuers of righteousness. Such a desire to please Him is the mark of every genuine believer.

John MacArthur

Though we are bound by time here on earth, we are actually living in eternity. Therefore, let us lift our eyes to the heavens and praise and worship our Lord God, who is from everlasting to everlasting.

Sheila Cragg

When Christ, who is your life, appears, then you also will appear with him in glory.

Colossians 3:4

Then I looked and heard the voice of many angels, numbering thousands upon thousands, and ten thousand times ten thousand. They encircled the throne and the living creatures and the elders. In a loud voice they sang: "Worthy is the Lamb, who was slain, to receive power and wealth and wisdom and strength and honor and glory and praise!"

Revelation 5:11-12

Our Creator is molding and shaping us, like clay in the hands of a master potter, moment by moment—and His Word promises that He will faithfully complete the work He has begun in us. Each day we encounter brings us closer to that longed-for instant when we will see Jesus face to face as we join Him in eternity.

Debra Evans

So where is this glory, this better country? It is a place where each moment is better than the last, reaching to eternity. Because of the Light that outshines the sun, the darkness of evil shall never have a place there.

Until we get to this glory, we are bombarded with temptations to settle for mere earthly, passing beauty. But such a fraudulent trade comes at a price: We lose the assurance of God's promises; His Word becomes less of a priority and thus less of a joy; our security in God gets traded for things of far less value. . . .

The most damaging thing this seduction can do is make us forget our whole reason for living here on planet earth. We were created not to pursue the comfortable life, but to care for people the way God does.

Donna Morley

verlasting life is something to which I look forward. Why? Not because I am out of love with life here—just the reverse! My life is full of joy, from four sources—knowing God, and people, and the good and pleasant things that God and men under God have created, and doing things which are worthwhile for God or others, or for myself as God's man. But my reach exceeds my grasp. My relationships with God and others are never as rich and full as I want them to be, and I am always finding more than I thought was there in great music, great verse, great books, great lives, and the great kaleidoscope of the natural order.

As I get older, I find that I appreciate God, and people, and good and lovely and noble things, more and more intensely; so it is pure delight to think that this enjoyment will continue and increase in some form (what form, God knows, and I am content to wait and see), literally forever. Christians inherit in fact the destiny that fairy tales envisage in fancy: we (yes, you and I, the silly saved sinners) live, and live happily, and by God's endless mercy will live happily ever after.

We cannot visualize heaven's life, and the wise man will not try. Instead, he will dwell on the doctrine of heaven, which is that there the redeemed will find all their heart's desire: joy with their Lord, joy with His people, and joy in the ending of all frustration and distress and the supply of all wants. . . .

Often now we say in moments of great enjoyment, "I don't want this ever to stop"—but it does. Heaven, however, is different. May heaven's joy be yours, and mine.

J. I. PACKER

[The] intangible needs of our soul will never be fully met this side of eternity. God Himself "has also set eternity in the hearts of men" (Ecclesiastes 3:11). He's written the Story of eternal transcendent things in our hearts. . . . This deep connection with the Author and His Story compels us to long for God's justice . . . to long for His freedom, His peace, complete healing and restoration for broken relationships and broken homes. No more war, poverty, disease, or pain.

Lael F. Arrington

Most North American Christians have things so good right here in this world that they don't really know what it is to long for heaven. God has blessed us with an abundance of earthly comforts—more than any prior generation in history. There is a danger that we become so comfortable in this life that we forget we are but strangers and pilgrims in this world. Like Abraham, we're supposed to think of ourselves as vagabonds here on earth, looking for a city with eternal foundations, whose builder and maker is God (Hebrews 11:10).

John MacArthur

There are many rooms in my Father's home, and I am going to prepare a place for you.

John 14:2 NLT

a bright
tomorrow

He who stands firm to the end will be saved. And this gospel of the kingdom will be preached in the whole world as a testimony to all nations, and then the end will come.

Matthew 24:13-14

As believers we have the promise of a glorious inheritance. . . . We are promised an inheritance that will never spoil or fade, a place of peace and rest, a place within the Father's house where He will wipe away every tear from our eyes. We are promised the inheritance of eternal life. We are heirs of the hope of heaven.

David Haney

God has planned something far better for us than what this earth holds. Jesus is preparing a place for us, an eternal home in heaven where we will enjoy the rewards of dwelling forever with Him (John 14:2-3).

Sheila Cragg

I suppose that most middle-class Americans of the Baby Boomer generation share my memories of Christmas, or more precisely, the memories of the hours before Christmas morning. These were some of the longest hours in my life. During the time of anticipation before the gift-giving orgy on Christmas morning, each minute seemed a lifetime. Even though I was exiled to my bedroom for the final hours before sunrise, sleep was impossible. In all of my childhood experience, I never knew such anticipation. Patience was not a virtue to me during these hours; it was a curse. . . .

Isn't this the attitude we should have toward heaven? If the glory of eternity, the presence of Christ, and the reunion of the saints are not our most anticipated moments, then what are? Is not our discomfort with the wait an expression of our longing and our hope? Shouldn't we be scratching and clawing at the gates of heaven, anxious for them to open?

David Haney

God not only created us to be homesick for loved ones and home but for Himself and heaven. "You have made us for yourself, and our heart is restless until it rests in you" [wrote Augustine].

Sheila Cragg

Heaven will feel like home to us—the place where we belong (Philippians 3:20).

Ellen Banks Elwell

We American Christians need to remember, as Os Guinness has said, that our glory days are not in the past. Rather, our golden era lies in the future. We will celebrate and rejoice in the end of the Story, no matter how our part plays out.

Lael F. Arrington

Many of us can't enjoy the Christian life because we are thinking about how much fun the world used to be. We're thinking about the garlic and leeks back in Egypt, and we are stuck out here in the wilderness with manna.

Well, I'm here to tell you that if you start thinking like that, you're looking at forty years of aimless wandering in your Christian pilgrimage. The person of faith is looking to tomorrow, as hard and as far away as it may look. Biblical faith says, "God, I am looking at Your tomorrow." Now what's back there may be enticing. Back there may be a lot of fun and old friends. But God isn't back there. . . . God is in your future.

Are you being tempted to look back or even go back today? Claim the promises of God, anticipate them, look ahead to God's future for you. Look ahead to where He's taking you.

Tony Evans

I am sure of this one truth: No one will go to heaven except by the grace of God and through the merits of the blood of Jesus Christ.

Ray Pritchard

What shall we do in heaven? Not lounge around but worship, work, think, communicate, and enjoy activity, beauty, people, and God. First and foremost, however, we shall see and love Jesus, our Savior, Master, and Friend.

J. I. Packer

But our citizenship is in heaven. And we eagerly await a Savior from there, the Lord Jesus Christ, who, by the power that enables him to bring everything under his control, will transform our lowly bodies so that they will be like his glorious body.

Philippians 3:20-21

Therefore you do not lack any spiritual gift as you eagerly wait for our Lord Jesus Christ to be revealed. He will keep you strong to the end, so that you will be blameless on the day of our Lord Jesus Christ. God, who has called you into fellowship with his Son Jesus Christ our Lord, is faithful.

1 Corinthians 1:7-9

A sweeping technicolor vision of heaven inspires ordinary people to do extraordinary, heroic things. The heroes of the "Hall of Faith" prized their heavenly citizenship above all the creature comforts of home. By faith they were certain of what they could not see—a "city with foundations whose architect and builder is God" (Hebrews 11:10). Many of these were quite wealthy—Abraham, Jacob, Joseph, Moses in Pharaoh's court—but they held their earthly gains lightly. "They admitted . . . they were longing for a better country—a heavenly one" (Hebrews 11:13, 16).

Lael F. Arrington

This is the promise of resurrection. If Jesus was raised by the Spirit, and that exact same Spirit lives in us, then that exact same Spirit will also one day raise us. We have a hope of a future resurrection because of one that happened in the past, and the team that pulled off the first one is the same team that will pull off the future one. Count on it. This is what we are hoping for, and it is not an unfounded hope. . . .

We are secure in knowing that the Spirit who lives within us keeps His promises. We are secure because there is nothing, not even death, that He cannot conquer.

David Haney

Heaven is His realm. He has gone there to prepare a place for us to live with Him forever. That truth is what makes heaven so precious for the Christian. Our eternity there will be an eternity in the presence of Christ, sharing rich fellowship with Him personally and living endlessly in the light of His countenance. That is heaven's chief appeal for the Christian whose priorities are straight. Christ Himself is the glory of heaven.

John MacArthur

As we look around the corridors of heaven and search through the reaches of eternity, the glory of our redemption will be the most spectacular aspect of heaven. Of all the creatures and all the magnificent creation that we will enjoy in eternity, the greatest instrument of God's glory will be ourselves. As we are reunited with those we love, as we see the lives of those who have been touched by our own, as we travel throughout heaven, His glory will be revealed not only to us but also by us. We are the agents and audience of God's glory.

David Haney

Our citizenship is in heaven, according to Philippians 3:20. In other words, heaven is where we belong.

John MacArthur

uotations are taken from the Bible and from the following Crossway books:

Arrington, Lael F., *Worldproofing Your Kids*
Carmichael, Nancie, *Desperate for God*
_____, *Your Life, God's Home*
Carson, D. A., *For the Love of God,* Vol. 2
Cragg, Sheila, *A Woman's Journey Toward Holiness*
_____, *A Woman's Pilgrimage of Faith*
_____, *A Woman's Walk with God*
Elliff, Tom, *A Passion for Prayer*
Elwell, Ellen Banks, *Quiet Moments of Encouragement for Moms*
_____, *Quiet Moments of Faith for Moms*
_____, *Quiet Moments of Hope for Moms*
_____, *Quiet Moments of Wisdom for Moms*
Evans, Debra, *Christian Woman's Guide to Sexuality, The*
Evans, Tony, *No More Excuses*
_____, *Time to Get Serious*
Ford, Cheryl V., *Pilgrim's Progress Devotional, The*
Ganz, Richard L., *Secret of Self-Control, The*
Guinness, Os, *God in the Dark*
Haney, David, *A Living Hope*
Hughes, R. Kent, *Abba Father*
_____, *Disciplines of a Godly Man*
_____, *Disciplines of Grace*
Hunt, Susan, *By Design*
James, Mary D., *Praise! Our Songs and Hymns*
Lawson, Steven J., *Faith Under Fire*
_____, *Final Call*
Lloyd-Jones, Martyn, *Revival*
MacArthur, John F., *Drawing Near*
_____, *Glory of Heaven, The*
_____, *In the Footsteps of Faith*
_____, *Nothing but the Truth*
_____, *Pillars of Christian Character, The*
_____, *Power of Integrity, The*
_____, *Second Coming, The*

Bibliography

Macaulay, Susan Schaeffer, *For the Family's Sake*
Mason, Mike, *The Gospel According to Job*
Meyer, F. B., quoted in *Into His Presence*
Morley, Donna, *Choices That Lead to Godliness*
Moule, H. C. G., quoted in *Into His Presence*
Olford, Stephen F., *Not I but Christ*
_____, *Way of Holiness, The*
Ortlund, Jr., Raymond C., *A Passion for God*
Packer, J. I., *Growing in Christ*
_____, *A Passion for Faithfulness*
_____, *A Quest for Godliness*
Palms, Roger C., *An Unexpected Hope*
Patton, William W., quoted in *Into His Presence*
Ryken, Philip Graham, *Courage to Stand*
_____, *Discovering God in Stories from the Bible*
Piper, John, *A Hunger for God*
_____, *Legacy of Sovereign Joy, The*
Pippert, Rebecca Manley, *A Heart Like His*
Pritchard, Ray, *Man of Honor*
_____, *Road Best Traveled, The*
_____, *What a Christian Believes*
Rogers, Adrian, *Lord Is My Shepherd, The*
_____, *Power of His Presence, The*
Schaeffer, Edith, *Art of Life, The*
_____, *Life of Prayer, The*
Schaeffer, Francis A., *Finished Work of Christ, The*
_____, *Letters of Francis A. Schaeffer*
Spurgeon, C. H., quoted in *Into His Presence*
Warner, Timothy M., *Spiritual Warfare*

STEPS TO PEACE WITH GOD

1. **RECOGNIZE GOD'S PLAN—PEACE AND LIFE**

   The message you have read in this book stresses
   that God loves you and wants you to
   experience His peace and life.

   The BIBLE says ... *"For God loved the
   world so much that He gave His only Son,
   so that everyone who believes in Him may
   not die but have eternal life." John 3:16*

2. **REALIZE OUR PROBLEM—SEPARATION**

   People choose to disobey God and go
   their own way. This results in separation
   from God.

   The BIBLE says ... *"Everyone has sinned
   and is far away from God's saving presence." Romans 3:23*

3. **RESPOND TO GOD'S REMEDY—CROSS OF CHRIST**

   God sent His Son to bridge the gap. Christ
   did this by paying the penalty of our sins
   when He died on the cross and rose from
   the grave.

   The BIBLE says ... *"But God has shown
   us how much He loves us—it was while we
   were still sinners that Christ died for us!"
   Romans 5:8*

   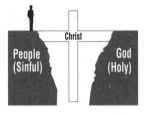

4. **RECEIVE GOD'S SON—LORD AND SAVIOR**

   You cross the bridge into God's family
   when you ask Christ to come into your life.

   The BIBLE says ... *"Some, however, did
   receive Him and believed in Him; so He
   gave them the right to become God's
   children." John 1:12*

   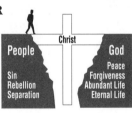

THE INVITATION IS TO:
REPENT (turn from your sins) and by faith RECEIVE Jesus Christ into your
heart and life and follow Him in obedience as your Lord and Savior.

PRAYER OF COMMITMENT
"Lord Jesus, I know I am a sinner. I believe You died for my sins. Right now, I
turn from my sins and open the door of my heart and life. I receive You as
my personal Lord and Savior. Thank You for saving me now. Amen."

If you want further help in the decision you have made, write to:
Billy Graham Evangelistic Association, P.O. Box 779, Minneapolis, MN 55440-0779